PENGUIN BOOKS

SH*TSHOW!

Charlie LeDuff is a Pulitzer Prize–winning journalist, formerly at the *New York Times*, the *Detroit News*, and Detroit's Fox 2 News. The author of *Detroit, US Guys*, and *Work and Other Sins*, he lives near Detroit.

ALSO BY CHARLIE LeDUFF

*Detroit*

*US Guys*

*Work and Other Sins*

# Sh*tshow!

## THE COUNTRY'S COLLAPSING . . . AND THE RATINGS ARE GREAT

## CHARLIE LeDUFF

PENGUIN BOOKS

PENGUIN BOOKS
An imprint of Penguin Random House LLC
penguinrandomhouse.com

First published in the United States of America by Penguin Press,
an imprint of Penguin Random House LLC, 2018
Published with a new afterword by the author in Penguin Books 2019

Portions of this book appeared in different form in *Mother Jones,*
*The New York Times,* and *Vice News.*

ISBN 9780525522041 (paperback)

THE LIBRARY OF CONGRESS HAS CATALOGED THE
HARDCOVER EDITION AS FOLLOWS:
Library of Congress Cataloging-in-Publication Data
Names: LeDuff, Charlie, author.
Title: Sh*tshow! : the country's collapsing—and the ratings are
great / Charlie LeDuff.
Other titles: Shitshow | Shit show
Description: New York : Penguin Press, [2018]
Identifiers: LCCN 2018006192 (print) | LCCN 2018031458 (ebook) |
ISBN 9780525522034 (ebook) | ISBN 9780525522027 (hardcover)
Subjects: LCSH: United States—Social conditions—21st century. | United States—
Economic conditions—21st century. | United States—Race relations—History—21st
century. | United States—Politics and government—2009–2017. | United States—
Civilization—21st century.
Classification: LCC HN59.2 (ebook) | LCC HN59.2 .L44 2018 (print) |
DDC 306.0973—dc23
LC record available at https://lccn.loc.gov/2018006192

Printed in the United States of America
1   3   5   7   9   10   8   6   4   2

*Designed by Amanda Dewey*

# Contents

**2013**

# Red, White & Rog

I'd arrived full of piss and tonic, ready to pitch Roger Ailes my idea for a national TV news segment called *The Americans,* but the morguelike atmosphere dampened my enthusiasm. The Fox News offices in Manhattan were a warren of cubicles with shitty fluorescent lighting and drab, yellowing paint. People were cowed and hollow-eyed behind their cheap modular desks, tap-tap-tapping numbly on their keyboards. Bill O'Reilly scuttled through the lobby, scowling and distracted. He looked like hell without makeup, saggy bottomed, squeezed like an old dishrag.

Papa Bear! I shouted to him, fist in the air, fight-the-power-like.

He threw a sour, dismissive wave and shambled on toward the elevator bank. There he went: No Spin Bill, carrying the weight of the country's number one cable news show on those seductive, sloping shoulders. Give 'em hell, Papa Bear!

Roger Ailes, the president of Fox News, had a nice office, his door kept sentinel by a young bombshell with black stockings and skirt and a tight sweater, put together like the bevy of other young bombshells with black stockings and ample cleavage who populated this Fox News mother ship, tap-tap-tapping. Who created this Plasticine paradise? Who was the genius who came up with the concept to marry family values with unquenched geriatric libido?

I was escorted into Ailes's inner sanctum, chaperoned by two senior Fox executives.

This Ailes, by the look of things, he knew how. A large, understated office. A window facing uptown. A couch. A private toilet. A desk with absolutely no paper on it. Nothing. No schedules. No contracts. No tissue. No disposable cup. No lint.

It's all done right here, said The Rog, pinched and slightly rotund, tapping his pale, bald skull with an index finger. The map of the kingdom was carried in his head.

Roger is a genius, explained one of the executives who brought me to meet the Exalted. He built this from scratch and he keeps the recipe to himself.

My stars don't like it, Rog said, but I go by instinct. How are my stars? They don't like the new schedule?

Stars, I thought. He called his commentators stars.

Well, I'm a local TV reporter for your Fox station in Detroit, I said.

I know, he responded, pointing to his magical skull. You wrote a book.

Yes, well, like I said in the book, Mr. Ailes, Detroit is not its own little freak show. The whole country is bankrupt and on high boil. It's a shitshow out there. What I'd like to do is a series of dispatches for your local television group [Fox directly owned eighteen local stations in America's biggest markets, usually one with an NFL team]. Go across America with a camera, show what's really going on between L.A. and New York. Get in touch with the real people. They're missing from your airwaves, you know. And the election's coming sooner than you think.

Rog looked at his executives and asked: Can we control him?

What the fuck is that supposed to mean? I asked him just like that because Rog was no shrinking violet. He was battle-tested. He'd been around the barracks with that upper-plate smile, crooked and dangerous, his eyes glazed, unhealthy, and bulbous. You just knew you could talk to Rog, the man who created the "Richard Nixon Show" and then went on to create bullshit right-wing TV news. Rog was the man who realized there was a tremendous audience of people out there who were tired of the decades of bullshit left-wing news they were being fed. So Rog was a genius.

Now, I was proposing something down-up and right down the middle, something showcasing everyday people who were trying to get by as the country and their way of life disintegrated around them.

I don't want you going off and doing stories on Rupert Murdoch's charities, he said gravely.

What the wizard was telling me was that he didn't want stories that would cost him money or advertisers or instigate phone calls from the country club or from The Boss himself. These were the same concerns of liberal media executives. In the end, news isn't really about keeping the public informed or holding the powerful to account. It's about cash money. The First Amendment is a fine thing, but the Founding Fathers didn't think to leave the media a revenue stream. That's why the industry pushes as many stories as it does about doped-up starlets, foil-hat crackpots, and cats, so many cats—runaway cats, talking cats, ghost cats, cats on the toilet, amputee cats in wheelchairs. Money made the twenty-four-hour news cycle spin round. I'd learned that much in my years as a newspaperman.

And frankly, what did I care about Rupert's charities? I mean, I'm no collaborator, no corporate lap dog. I'm not a tool or an organ or a megaphone for the ruling class. I don't do drinks or retreats or White House Correspondents' Dinners. Proximity to power does nothing for me. I don't even call myself a journalist. Reporter, straight up. But I can't imagine anything as arcane as Rupert's charities. I'll leave that to the chattering chimps and op-ed writers. I just wanted to get into the dirt of American life.

All right, he said straight from his famous gut. We'll give it a shot.

To his credit, Rog was straight up about it. There was no "turn around and let me get a look at you." No feeling up my pectorals or biceps. No invitation to a boozy luncheon at a high-end hotel. None of the alleged harassment that three years later would lead to Ailes's ouster from the network he had built. It's much easier to get hired in TV news—especially if you have a limited intellectual skill set—if you're primped and powdered and physically possessed. Bad hair and yellow teeth don't get you very far. But Rog saw beyond it. Ailes said yes to me and the show, and I owe him much gratitude for that.

What you have in your hands is a chronology of those stories charting three years I traveled the country as a TV reporter for a segment on *The Americans* that aired across the country; three years of significant change to the American political, racial, and economic landscape. From the obvious and not-so-obvious effects of the new globalism to the growing strife between black and white, between the people and a government they feel has abandoned and cheated them. I did my damnedest to get up close and personal, to understand people and their very real anxieties and desperation. The American dream was slipping away, I knew that. Mortgaged down the river. But what, besides social media, part-time work, and prescription medication, was replacing it?

Black Lives Matter. The Sagebrush Rebellion. The poisoning of Flint. The ascendance of Trump. These events and conflagrations will very likely be remembered as pivotal moments in modern American history. And we were there, on the ground and in the tear gas with our cameras and notebooks, no makeup.

Watching the unspooling of America from the street corners and the corner bars, listening to the people's desire for something new, I was not surprised by the rise of President Donald J. Trump, and through the events in this book I hope to show you why. He and the traveling circus seals of media dovetailed spectacularly into our shitshow and we used them as side props for all they were worth.

At a press conference before he addressed an overflowing crowd near Flint early in his candidacy, for instance, I told Trump that I thought he could win the whole thing. He just needed to *say* things better. Frame them in a common language that wouldn't trigger a race war. Trump swelled like a thirsty sponge, pleased with my assessment of his chances, marveling at my astuteness and credibility as a journalist. As a follow-up, I asked him to consider my credentials before he settled on a running mate for vice president.

The question confused him for a moment.

You want to be vice president?

Sure. Why not?

Now he shifted gears. He challenged my credibility. He asked where I'd come from. Like, *who let this guy in here?* Now he turned to the room. Where did *he* come from?

The media laughed at me. It was the only time I ever heard Trump and a room full of reporters agree on anything.

I didn't actually want to be his running mate; it was meant as performance art with the presidential candidate serving as a midway sideshow in the American carnival we were broadcasting into your living room. The new journalism of the twenty-first century, in my mind, required not only literal brains and figurative balls, it also required style and presentation, hyperbole and humor, ostentation and outrage. But above all, it had to be accurate.

TV news is quite probably the most superficial form of journalism ever invented. Hunter Thompson characterized it fifty years ago as a long plastic hallway where thieves and pimps run free and good men go to die. I can report with certainty that little has changed but the faces on the screen.

These pages are populated with the stories of the men and women of America, and I dedicate this book to them. Cops, Marines, cowboys, Indians, immigrants, factory workers, barbers, pig farmers, housewives, widows, smugglers, pickpockets, politicians and other thieves, the Latino gardener who mows the lawn of the Grand Dragon of the KKK: They're all here along with those struggling under the burden of debt and underemployment who have been ignored too long and have had to make unsavory choices just to feed the children. This book is dedicated to all of them—except the Grand Dragon. That man can kiss my ass.

B ack in the office with Rog now, our business done, he segued neatly into talk about firearms.

You like guns?

Sure, I said. You come in my house uninvited, I'll waste you. I promise you that.

He liked the sentiment. He smiled, showing me his concealed-weapons permit, the executives forbidding me from tweeting a photograph of it. I asked him to sign my American flag boots, just as I do of every crazy I meet, from congressman to Frisco crack whore to middleweight champion of the world. Rog took my Sharpie and reached for my left boot.

Sign the right boot, Rog, I instructed him. The *far* right. That's it. Yes sir.

With the cap back on the pen, the executives preceded me out the door while Rog veered toward his barren desk. I stopped and tried the door off to the left. It was Rog's personal toilet, and I needed to take a dump. Too much coffee. I was going to be the wild-man national correspondent in the worst form of communication ever invented, local TV news (albeit in eighteen cities), and I was going to start by depositing a No. 2 in the No. 1's castle. Hell, I might even tweet it. I didn't even have time to get my belt undone before the secretary politely stopped me.

I'm sorry, she whispered, Mr. Ailes is very particular about his toilet. It's off-limits to everyone without an invitation. I'm sure you understand.

Yes, yes, I'm sure I do. I do understand. An invitation. Yes, thank you.

In the end, I might not have been sexy enough to earn my way into Rog's million-dollar water closet, but I had a show, and it was time to hit the road.

# 2014

I thought our first story should be about work. More than five years after the global economic collapse, people in the United States were still struggling to find it. Slews of them had headed for what was billed as a modern-day gold rush: the North Dakota oil fields.

The epicenter of the boom was a town named Williston, located on the Missouri River in the northwestern corner of the state.

The town sits in the ancestral lands of Sacajawea, and from the first days the white man paddled in, records reveal a history of venality, misunderstandings, hurt feelings, and a crippling lack of female companionship. One need look no further than the account of William Clark, co-captain of the Lewis and Clark Expedition.

On November 22, 1804, while camped north of modern-day Bismarck, Clark noted in his diary that an Indian woman had come into the camp who had been beaten and stabbed by her husband. The husband, it seems, was on the verge of killing her for sleeping with one of the expedition's sergeants without her husband's consent.

"I went down and spoke to the fellow about the rash act he was *likely to commit," Clark wrote, "and forbade any act of the kind near the Fort . . . We directed that no man of this party have any intercourse with this woman under the penalty of punishment . . . We directed the sergeant to give [the husband] some articles, at which time I told the Indian that I believed not one man of the party had touched his wife except the one he had [previously] given the use of her for a night, in his own bed . . . and advised him to take his squaw home and live happily together in future. At this time the grand chief of the nation arrived, and lectured him, and they both went off, apparently dissatisfied."*

*Venality and lack of female companionship. That was as good and honest a news report from the oil fields of North Dakota as I had read. We packed our bags for an update, looking for the American dream. Boomtown beckoned.*

# Black Gold

A shitty room near Fort Berthold, halfway between Minot and Williston, was going for $250 a night, minimum. A bunk mate would cost you an extra $50. But you could barely get a room anyway, because the joint was so jammed. Bob and Matt, my two camera guys, and I managed to snatch the last room. They took the single beds. I rolled a bag out on the floor, which was sticky and smelled like sewage and slag. A literal cracker box, this place, packed to the lip with white men from Alabama, Mississippi, Texas, Idaho looking for a last chance. Out-of-work men trying to hold the marriage together. Trying to keep the house back home. They were told there were jobs up here in the oil fields: ten billion barrels waiting to be fracked out of the shale deep below the frozen Dakota plains.

Rumor was these were good-paying jobs where a man could pull down a hundred grand in a year. All humps welcome, and all humps came.

A hundred grand! That would make the old lady happy, said one of the good ol' boys as he smoked a menthol and sipped on a Bud Light in the frozen parking lot of the shitbox motel that evening. That'd keep her from taking the kids and walking away, or, worse, leaving the kids and walking away.

Good ol' boy wasn't staying in the motel, he said, 'cause the talk about all that money was a lie. His explanation went like this: You'd make the hun'red grand alright, if you could find the work. But even if you found the work, you're working a hun'red hours a week and the work ain't steady 'cause so many good ol' boys with a nutsack packed their trucks and stomped the accelerator and barreled due north to this wild wasteland hoping for one last chance.

So without the money, this good ol' boy was sleeping in his truck in the parking lot, despite the fact it was January and minus forty-five outside with the wind blowing. And even then, he had to pay the night clerk twenty bucks for the privilege of a parking space. Just be gone by sunup before the manager showed up.

They found a body out there, he went on, throwing his chin toward the darkness that marked the edge of town. In a ditch out there, past where the lights run out. Wrapped in a mattress. Shot in the head. Frozen. Mexican guy. What the fuck are Mexicans doing all the way up here?

Mexicans? They're like the modern-day Chinese, I told him. They'll go anywhere. Go to the Congo, there's a Chinese restaurant. Detroit, Chinese restaurant. If your guts are rumbling with emptiness, you'll pretty much go anywhere. Kind of like you, I said.

Dunno, he mumbled. All's I know is there's a frozen fucking burrito in a ditch out there. This place is wild, son. It sucks. I can't wait to get a little bankroll and get the fuck gone.

Back inside the motel, the stench had changed like an olfactory mood ring. It now reeked of stale sweat and oil, smoke and rotten beer. Someone in a room down the hall was shrieking and it was blowing through the thin plasterboard, but no one said a thing. Someone got some bad meth. Or good meth. Hard to tell. Drug-induced paranoia is just one degree away from euphoria. Best not to open the door in any case. Best to have a beer and monitor the madman, in case he came crashing through the thin walls or started shooting the place up. Matt went to sleep with a pillow over his head. Bob snored over the ruckus. I lay awake, shivering on the floor, listening to the lunatic howl until dawn.

The morning sun came late. White and dead. Ice crystals sparkled on the prairie grass. No trees. Bold, rugged tundra. Fort Berthold was on the way to the burgeoning town of Williston, the epicenter of the Bakken Formation, which was said to be producing more oil than any other place in America, even Alaska's Arctic Circle. About a third of that production came from Fort Berthold, the once impoverished Indian reservation that was a little less impoverished now but nevertheless impoverished—home to the Three Affiliated Tribes, the Mandan, Hidatsa, and Arikara, the adopted people of Sacajawea. Over the years, the tribes had seen their territory whittled down by white theft to less than a million acres. First came the ranchers, then the railroads, and finally, in 1953, the Army Corps of Engineers, who dammed the Missouri River, flooding 150,000 acres of the best land and forcing the Indians onto the rugged, barren foothills. Funny thing about rugged, barren foothills. They tend to contain gold and uranium and oil.

Across the rolling hills of the rez, methane gas flares from fracking wells leased to white-man wildcatters blew like Roman candles. But little of the money they generated seemed be making its way to the people of the Affiliated Tribes, who had sued, claiming the federal government facilitated the theft of more than $1 billion by failing in its legal obligation to make sure the tribe was looked after. White speculators and New York hedge funds were buying up leasing rights for a song: $35 an acre.

The rez had become an ecological wasteland of oil spills and trucking roads and filthy air, and it was unclear what effect the polymers pumped down to break the oil shale might have on the health of the Missouri River above. Think about that whenever you see the blue flames of a cooking stove.

To make matters worse, the white man also claimed right-of-way for an oil and gas pipeline under the newly created sacred Lake Sakakawea. If they had known then what their land would look like today, I'm sure the natives would have slit Lewis's and Clark's throats, severed their hairy heads, and floated them back down the Missouri River to St. Louis.

But that was all water under the bridge. These days, the tribal government was like the white man's government—rotten, self-serving, kleptomaniacal. Tex Hall, the tribe's chairman, had been helping himself with a lucrative oil-services business on the side, pairing up with a white businessman who had a long, violent rap sheet in Oregon. As we were driving through North Dakota, it hit the local papers that Hall's white man was suspected of two business-related murders for hire, one in Spokane, Washington, and one right there on the reservation, on Hall's property no less, the victim bludgeoned to death in the chairman's garage, the theory went. Something about an argument over an oil lease. Authorities believe his body was buried out in the oil fields. While Hall's white partner was convicted in 2016 in the man's slaying, Hall denied involvement in the crime and to date has never been directly implicated.

As for Tex Hall's perfidy? Fattening himself while supposedly representing people who straggled around sucking dirty air and who on average died before they were able to collect Social Security?

Well, there was nothing in the tribal constitution that forbade it, the most august sachem told the newspapers. Sovereignty by the barrel, he declared.

The receptionist at the drab tribal government offices told me the chairman did not wish to speak to media that day. The chairman was at once ill and overwhelmed attending to the welfare of his great nation.

Hmmm. I have an appointment, I reminded her. I've come a long way.

I'm sorry.

I'm Native too. Ojibwe. Does that count for anything?

I'm sorry, the chairman is not available.

That's a strange name for an Indian chief, I said, showing my annoyance. Tex.

His native name is Red-Tipped Arrow, she explained. Nevertheless, as I've said, the chairman is not available and cannot see you right now.

In the middle of the rez, past the oil derricks and tractor-trailers and white men trudging around in canvas freezer suits manning the oil pumps, was a bridge that spanned the sacred artificial lake. From there, you could see a shining example of the chairman's magnanimity, his gift to his people, the fantastic development project purchased with oil money that would bring his ancient tribe into the twenty-first century. Past the casino, and there, right near the bait shop. A new hospital? you ask. A factory? A vocational school? No. A two-deck party yacht on cinder blocks, the *Island Girl*. Cost? Two and a half million dollars. She was supposed to be a casino boat, a gem that would make the reservation a tourist destination as well as an oil field. Problem is, someone forgot to remind Commodore Tex that the lake has been freezing over since 1953. Sovereignty by the barrel.

. . .

Williston, the white burg to the west of Fort Berthold, was being called the fastest-growing town in America. The neon
and asphalt and construction equipment were testament to a population that had doubled in five years to twenty-five thousand people. But that was only a measure of the people who actually stayed
in Williston and put down roots. It didn't include the huge transient
population of desperate men looking to pop in, strike it rich, and
hightail it home. Partly as a result of that influx, this once sleepy
town of Methodist churches and tidy brick homes now had the pre-
vailing character of a dirty hooker working at a truck stop near the
end of town.

And chances were you would find dirty hookers at the truck
stops between the Holiday Inn and the Kentucky Fried Chicken and
the El Rancho Hotel and the pop-up man-camps and the impromptu
trailer parks at the edge of town. The word was, a new millionaire
was minted in North Dakota every month. But where did these mag-
nates live? Where were their mansions? Their penthouses?

A local radio evangelist—I heard him on the AM dial while driving across the plains—was preaching about toothpaste tubes at
Kennedy Airport security and the lack of humanity in New York
and the need to trust in Jesus here on the oil patch. Jesus brings
inner peace, as well as a *piece of the pie.* I heard this and knew I had
to meet this man of divine perceptions.

Preacher Ron Evitt lived in a simple colonial in a neighborhood
of worn and stained aluminum siding. The son of a door-to-door
Gideon Bible salesman, Evitt studied petroleum engineering at the
University of Wyoming. He bought land with credit cards in the
early aughts, hit oil, and became a rich man. And with the price of a
barrel of crude at $107.57, he was getting richer with every upstroke

of the horse head. But money wasn't enough. The preacher desired souls, men, followers, acolytes, ratings! Yes, a slice of the Nielsen cake. What does it profit a man to gain the whole world if his show can't outperform NPR in Red State Country? The Preacher in the Patch—Oil Patch, that is—was his catchy tag out. But even so, the preacher found few ears for his paid radio spots—a few among the inmates at the county jail, a few druggies sleeping in their trucks, fewer still among the workers out at the wells. The well-hands lusted after money, not salvation.

We decided to film Evitt on a little proselytizing jaunt out to one of his wellheads. He brought pizza. People are more likely to sit and listen that way, he said. A little pepperoni adds spice to prayer.

The workers were all white men, and it dawned on me that I hadn't seen a solitary black man in North Dakota. Nor had I seen a Native man working in the oil fields. I had seen an Asian man cooking at a grubby Chinese restaurant in Minot, however. And there was that Mexican found in the culvert, wrapped in a spring mattress tortilla, sleeping the eternal sleep, but that's it.

We arrived at the wellhead with the preacher deep in the plains near the Canadian border. The winds had shifted, blowing in from the north now. It was blistering cold, so cold your fingers and toes burned and your face felt as if it had been scored with a sanding wheel. I had done time in slaughterhouses, but this had to be the toughest, most glum work I'd ever seen.

This ain't real work, said Bobby, a truck driver from Arkansas, as he waited to pump out fracking detritus from one of the preacher's holding tanks and dump it God knows where. This ain't the dream. This ain't the classic nine-to-five American dream. This is shit. You got to work nearly three full-time jobs if you want to make that hundred thousand. They don't tell you that before you come. You're tired. You're cold. You're beat down and lonely. A lot of guys don't have much experience on oil rigs or driving a truck, and that just makes the whole thing that much more dangerous.

He continued: The preacher? I just tell him "no thanks." I'm an atheist. There's no God. Look around. You see God? Me, my wife left. There's nothing for me back in Arkansas. I'm just trying to put a lump together. Buy me a shack in the woods in Idaho and disappear forever. That's all I want, a shack. That's my American dream.

Back in the workers' trailer, the preacher was working the men. He prayed, but they didn't. The pizza was swallowed, but the message wasn't.

The preacher, more Opie Taylor than Howard Hughes, with his bowl haircut and denim jacket, had little more success at the trailer park back near town. There were some families there, but it was single men mostly, bunking together, refusing to answer the door. Those that did bitterly informed the millionaire minister that they didn't need no prayers, they needed work. They needed money. The preacher said he would pray for them anyway, which was easy for him to do, since the preacher owned himself those couple of producing oil wells.

Looking around the shabby, snow-swept park with its invisible spirit of perdition and the legion of stay-at-homes and shut-ins and alcoholics, I thought: What had God wrought? I asked the preacher if he thought this is what the Lord and Savior Jesus Christ had in mind for men?

Yeah, well . . . the preacher fumbled. No, he finally admitted. Not really. Most of them aren't gonna find that dream.

I tracked down Williston's mayor, Ward Koeser, in his office in a shabby building off the main street not unlike the Indians' city hall: red brick made dull by soot and dust and mud kicked up by incessant semi-traffic. He was stepping down after twenty year in office.

He began with a don't-get-me-wrong preamble, which instantly made me think there was something wrong on the Great Plains. It's great, the mayor said. The development. The millions in construction. The new people.

Yeah, but?

But yes, there are the problems, all right. You're the media. You want to hear about the problems, right?

Well, yeah, right, I said, having been exposed. The good-news stuff is boring. Bad TV. Everybody's reported the production numbers and the mythological hundred grand. What about the meth and prostitution and homeless?

If it wouldn't be improper, the mayor said in a steady monotone, I would like to pay their way to go back where they came from.

Much of the rowdiness went on down by the rail station, the mayor told us. So naturally we went there. Down on Front Street, by the railroad tracks that ran parallel to the Missouri River, a mini–man-camp of trucks and RVs had sprung up. Before the oil rush, people didn't move to Williston, they moved away from it. But here they were, newcomers brought in by train or bus or wheezing vehicle, suffocating from desperation, without housing or companionship, sleeping in vans. Men shambling around down by the tracks. The hiring hall was here in Railroad Park, but it never seemed to be hiring. There was the Salvation Army, which occasionally dished out hot soup at noon, but you had to bow your head for it. Then there was the bus station and the train depot, a coffee shop and five bars on Main Street—two of them strip joints, Whispers and Heartbreakers.

Never one for idle gossip, I passed by Whispers and walked into Heartbreakers. It was simple to see why they called the place that. Four scruffy rummies at the rail. Animal busts on the wall. A mangy carpet. A mangy pole. A DJ booth. The TV was tuned to cable news. I don't know why they thought some chubby young white man wearing grandmother spectacles yammering on with the sound turned all the way down would be interesting to a strip joint full of desperadoes, but there it was. TV.

Someone had been stabbed outside Whispers recently, the lady bartender told me, assuring me at the same time that I was in the more classy establishment. People like to do that out west, I said, stabbing. Stabbing is much more neighborly, much more intimate and Christian than your basic drive-by shooting. That's city shit. Stab a guy in the eye, he sees it coming. That's the gentlemanly thing to do.

Oh, she said, giggling, we had someone shot and killed outside just a few months ago too. You get all kinds around here.

The bartender was a Mormon, from Idaho. She was a nicely put-together brunette. Halter top and short shorts, too cold for the weather, but a gal's got to advertise. Her daddy wasn't happy about her situation, she said, but what Daddy don't know . . .

Not that I'm that type of girl, I'm just the bartender. But there are some who can keep you company. Everybody needs company. A man is nothing but a stray without a companion. Three hundred dollars.

That's a lot of money for a few minutes in a mop closet, I said.

Price goes up when you smell. She tittered, tossing a thumb toward some greasy oilmen.

I went out for a cigarette to consider it. I was in it for the details, for the story, you understand, your intrepid reporter with his dispatch from the American dream. A $300 rumpus in a toilet stall in the train depot. Something about the image amused me. But you wouldn't be able to fob off something like that on an expense report.

Just then, a hobo living out of his truck called to me from his window, asking to mooch a cigarette. I went over. A Mexican guy! From Vegas. (Man, these Mexican dudes *will* go anywhere, just like the Chinese.) He told me he came out three months ago, worked for a little bit, but couldn't find nothing no more.

Police ran me out of the park, he said, so I'm sleeping down here, but the gas is getting low and I've got to keep the motor running all night or I'm going to freeze. So you see the problem I'm in, amigo? You see the problems I got? Gas runs out and I'm a Popsicle. So you understand, I'm not asking for a handout. Not asking for charity. I seen you come out of the club. Maybe you're a little lonely or something? I could suck your cock for twenty bucks. I'm not asking for charity or nothing. I'm willing to work for it. Twenty bucks?

Come again?

Okay, fifteen bucks? There was real hope in his voice.

What in Christ's name was this, preacher man? An angry, desperate backwater glowering orange and neon in the stinging night. Covered in mud and salt and ice, inhabited by gravel-lot hound dogs snarling on the chain, willing to lick your balls if a scoop of gravy came along with it. I didn't like this place. There was no American dream. Not here. We were all going to have to move on and keep looking.

No? All right, he said. Then thank you very much for the cigarillo. God bless. God bless. Yes sir. God bless. Say, listen, sorry to ask, but you got a little extra change? A little something? Another cigarette?

I felt bad for the guy. I didn't have the heart to tell him he was probably pricing himself well below market. At the rate he was going, that would be five thousand cocks before he reached the mythical hundred grand. I gave him ten bucks and another smoke.

Thank you, yes, *gracias*. I'm hoping to turn it around, a little luck. I'm expecting to hear back about a job tomorrow. If that happens, you know, then my troubles are over. A little luck, that is all that's needed.

*What's going on in this country? Unions stand against those trends. We've got to somehow insulate the robust American economy from this global economy that seems to want to devour our standard of living.*

—JAMES P. HOFFA, TEAMSTERS PRESIDENT

*No generation has ever had the opportunity that all of us now have to build a global economy that leaves no one behind. It is a wonderful opportunity.*

—FORMER U.S. PRESIDENT BILL CLINTON

*I've made this argument before, I'll make it again. We are part of a global economy. We're not reversing that.*

—FORMER U.S. PRESIDENT BARACK OBAMA

*This is a major day in Michigan's history. Again, I don't view this as anti-union at all. I believe it is pro-worker.*

—GOVERNOR RICK SNYDER

The American dream was dying. It was dying not only in Williston and the small towns from which the men there fled, but in the very place it was created.

It was a cold afternoon when thousands of union members were chanting on the capitol grounds as the outgoing Republican-led legislature voted to make Michigan the twenty-fourth right-to-work state in America. That meant a person who worked in a union shop *was not required to pay union dues but would still receive any benefits the union negotiated for its members. It was death for organized labor, which had been dying for years anyway. Even union members don't like paying dues. So who in his right mind would pay for something he could get for free?*

*The same thing was going on in Wisconsin with the public-sector employees. And like in Wisconsin, the governor of Michigan thought his coup de grâce against collective bargaining (pro-worker and freedom of choice was his preferred Orwellian phraseology) might be parlayed into a bid for the White House.*

*It was shocking, to Michigan union members at least, considering that the United Auto Workers was celebrating the seventy-fifth anniversary of its birth in Flint, just down the road.*

*It didn't take a fucking hundred years, one beefy protester lamented to me on the statehouse steps. His placard read "Union Til I Die."*

*I told him I hoped he still had his health care because death was coming sooner rather than later. He didn't laugh.*

*You think that's funny? he hissed. This is the North, motherfucker. This is Michigan, and they're turning us into fucking Mississippi.*

*Mississippi. He was close, but it wasn't exactly Mississippi.*

# The Blue, the Gray
# & the Green

Nestled in the rolling Alabama hills, among the shagbark and pine, somewhere between Tuscaloosa and Birmingham, is the sprawling Mercedes-Benz plant where three thousand non-union autoworkers assemble SUVs for soccer moms and slip-and-fall lawyers across the nation. An odd place to erect a factory, in the middle of nowhere. It's as if the company decided on the spot so that union sympathizers couldn't find it.

The truth is, they did put it here, way down in the southern pines, to dodge the unions. Alabama, Georgia, Tennessee, South Carolina, and yes, Mississippi. This region—the Sun Belt, they called it—was considered the new Detroit for foreign automakers. And over the last twenty years, nearly all the big manufacturers had planted their flags here: Volkswagen, BMW, Honda, Toyota,

Nissan, Hyundai. The problem for the United Auto Workers was that not a single one of these factories was a union shop. Since 1997, Mercedes-Benz has had a good thing going here in right-to-work Alabama. Why make it easy for the Yankees to stir the pot?

We pulled up on the shoulder of the road outside the Mercedes plant's main gate and decided to start filming some wide shots of the gargantuan facility, gleaming silver, oozing that multibillion-dollar, state-of-the-art grandeur that's hard, if not impossible, to find in the Rust Belt. But we barely got the tripods out of the van before company goons rolled up on us in Mercedes SUVs. Nice touch. We clearly reeked of strangeness—rental van, cameras, goatees. We must be pinkos, hippies, socialists maybe. Or worse, northern media elitists. Liberals. The security guard stepped out of his truck, put on his hat, adjusted his belt. A real Buford Pusser, this one. He radioed our plate number to dispatch, gave us the silent once-over, then demanded identification. Just like that. No "Afternoon, gentlemen." No "Howdy, boys." Just *Lemme see some IDs*.

I've got a lot of respect for the police. I was taught to respect the police early, when as a teenager a couple buddies and I decided to break into an empty wing of an apartment complex. We weren't B&E specialists, we weren't particularly good at it, but we weren't stealing anything either. Just smoking dope and drinking malt liquor when the cops arrived. I don't remember them asking for ID. They simply took us out back by the chain-link fence. And with a quick flurry of rabbit punches to the kidneys taught us some respect. I've always looked at it as a favor. A wake-up call. Punks like us tended to end up in prison, or, worse, living out their days in that very apartment complex next to the polluted river. I am fortunate enough as an adult to live in a house along the interstate, so I did better than expected considering the circumstances. And, as I said, I was taught to have respect for the police. I was taught to *comply*.

But I also have respect for the notion of probable cause and be-ing left the fuck alone. Once a punk, always a punk, the saying goes. But now I was a punk with a press badge.

(Disclaimer: It's a homemade press badge. Our employer, strangely, never issued press passes to its reporters. Maybe they didn't think it was necessary. Maybe the executives didn't believe we were actually doing real news. But credentials can be very im-portant when you're trying to gain access to halls of power, or when some hayseed in a trailer park needs to see something official to discourage him from stealing your equipment, or when some self-important mall cop tries to inflate his ego at your expense. Long story short, in lieu of real credentials, we pasted some company lo-gos to photographs of ourselves, then glued on a bar code from a snack-cake package, added some verbiage, NEWS MEDIA PRESS OF-FICIAL IDENTIFICATION, laminated it all, added a lanyard, and voilà! Press badge!)

But I digress. Back to Buford.

There was just something about the guy that rubbed me wrong. An unnecessary hard-ass. *Lemme see some IDs.* He was out of his jurisdiction, here on the highway. I wasn't going to show him shit.

By what authority? I asked him. (I laughed to myself envision-ing the job he *should* be doing: I think someone in the lunchroom forgot to recycle their soda can, Officer Ornery. Why don't you scamper off and look into that?)

You're trespassing, said the company man.

Again, he was wearing the type of hat state troopers do, but he wasn't one. Just another bully being paid ten bucks an hour to in-timidate people. The country's full of guys like him. A man's got to eat, I suppose. The American dream.

This is a public road, I told him.

You're impeding traffic.

We're on the shoulder, I countered to his counter. If we're impeding traffic, then call the police. The genuine police.

Listen, son.

Son? It's sir. You can call me sir, I said, waving my bullshit credentials.

Listen, son . . .

So we started filming the guy.

Go on, then, I said. Call the cops. We'll wait right here.

Bob, camera rolling, walked in a little tighter so the man could have his close-up.

I was getting used to the treatment. We'd gotten the same reception a day earlier, up in Chattanooga, Tennessee. Despite the UAW spending $5 million on a campaign to organize workers at the Volkswagen assembly plant there, the rank and file voted to reject the union, sending the carpetbaggers packing back north. It was a huge defeat. Chattanooga was supposed to be the first domino. Then the Mercedes plant, the crown jewel, would fall. It was supposed to be easy. Volkswagen executives, in true European fashion, sat neutral, even allowing the UAW access to the plant to organize. And still the union lost, leaving Tennessee only one of four non-union VW plants in the world, the others being in Russia and China.

Union bosses were blaming it on outside agitators bankrolled by the billionaire Koch brothers. Billboards near the interstate had popped up showing a decimated Packard automobile factory with the caption "Detroit. Brought to you by the UAW."

The Chamber of Commerce, U.S. senators, and even Tennessee's governor fought tooth and nail to keep the UAW out, threatening to pull the company's tax subsidies, spreading rumors around town that any future work—VW or otherwise—would go to Mexico. And yes, the rich man's minions were in Tennessee working the scene.

I met with one such man, who came up with that billboard, at the Starbucks off the highway. An urbane Manhattanite, skinny suit and dark glasses, so soft he'd probably bleed out if you socked him with a couch cushion. He was drinking a latte. He worked for a murky outfit called the Center for Worker Freedom, whose funding source he refused to disclose.

I love the working guy getting good wages, he insisted, explaining he was here precisely to look out for the working guy, make sure he didn't do something drastic like voting in a union, forcing the boss to move those wages and jobs down to Mexico. Just looking out for the little man's interests, is all.

How's that? I asked. You could blame technology for extinguishing some of the factory work in America, but if we hadn't signed NAFTA and WTO some of those jobs would still be here and the unions would have bargaining power. All that's left for many people are nine-dollar-an-hour strip mall jobs.

You don't have to make nine bucks an hour, he said, meaning you could find something better if you tried hard enough.

It was bullshit. Nine an hour, that's all that was left.

Latte Guy had nothing to add to that, because, really, now that the real estate hustle had imploded, all there was on the other side of the factory for a guy without a degree and increasingly even for a guy with a degree: drive-thru attendant.

But somehow we were expected to believe the stories put out by the union and parroted by the media that this scrawny latte guy was able to convince a whole factory of blue-collar southern auto-workers that banding together and collectively bargaining for better wages and work conditions was bad for them.

Really?

Or perhaps it was simply that the UAW never made its case to the southern folk, that it wasn't able to explain why there were now more Mexican autoworkers than there were American autoworkers. The workers here knew Michigan itself had recently become a right-to-work state and that the UAW had been powerless to stop it. Across the country, less than 7 percent of the private workforce belonged to a union. And they liked it that way.

Now what? What was the plan? Where was the road forward? When I went to UAW world headquarters in Detroit to ask, they tossed me off the lot. The union bosses in Chattanooga were instructed to go radio silent. VW had nothing of substance to say, but their goons too spied on us when we were talking to a group of workers outside the parking lot. The automobile culture, I was beginning to realize, is a hostile and surly one, secretive and paranoid, which explains the treatment one gets at the Department of Motor Vehicles office. So we made a beeline for Alabama, figuring we might be able to advance the story while all the attention was focused on Chattanooga.

U nnerved by the camera rolling on him, Major Hard-On from the Mercedes plant mumbled something about us hurrying up with our business, then drove off and parked behind the main gate with his headlights pointed toward the highway, trained on us. I'll give the guy credit, he took the job seriously.

I phoned a Mercedes worker I was scheduled to meet near the gates, telling him about the security guards and suggesting it was probably better to talk somewhere else unless he wanted to be stripped down to his underpants. It was arranged. But before we left, I leisurely did a couple stand-up lines into the camera, empty words and analysis we had no real intention of using. We just wanted to piss off the security goon.

My contact had picked a barbecue joint off a country road for our meet-up. Tim Earnest, like his name implies, was a simple, unpretentious middle-aged white man who'd been working happily in the Mercedes plant for more than a decade. He used to log a hundred driving miles from home to work, but still he saved his paycheck and bought a house closer to the plant. That old-time American dream. Work hard. Paid well. Save your money. Buy a house. Happy wife. Happy life.

Earnest brought along a group of equally modest coworkers who were against the union, including a woman who once, long ago, lived in the Detroit area.

It's pretty simple why they didn't want the UAW, Earnest explained. Did the union protect the workers at the Big Three, whose jobs were now in Mexico?

He was right. Where was their protection? What happened to their dues? The Germans, Earnest and his colleagues agreed, were good to work for. They paid twenty dollars an hour and provided health care and a 401(k). Why mess with that? Why agitate against a good thing? Where was the strategy in these new times? Why antagonize and give the company a reason to look toward Guadalajara?

You could blame right-wing agitators, or Tea Party congressmen, or the Koch brothers, but these working people had their own minds and their own reasons that, to me, made sense. Nobody here wanted to lose his job and have to pack his bags for North Dakota. They were making what their union counterparts were earning in the North, more or less. Why would you screw with what's good? Better to trust the German company than to bite it. All you had to do is look at Detroit or Janesville, Wisconsin, or any industrialized region in America to realize that the UAW—or any union, for that matter—was powerless to stop the march of globalization. What do you get for your dues? A couple hundred union bosses pulling down that mythical hundred grand whom you never met? The union spending your hard-earned money on political candidates you don't support? Candidates who never pushed anything but a pencil? No thank you, Bubba. Little difference between a Republican politician and a Democrat and a union boss as far as work goes. At least they say so here.

Bill Clinton signed NAFTA, you know, Earnest continued. Obama supports that big trade deal in Asia, you know. That doesn't work out real good for us working folk. It never does. I don't want a handout. Never took welfare. I just want to work. No, never mind the union. Nothing but trouble.

The local UAW organizers had a storefront office not too far from the restaurant, and I figured we'd give them a try. Now that Tennessee had gone up in flames, what was the plan with Alabama? I walked in. The organizers looked at each other and then at me in a panic. A few no-comments later, they put us out on the sidewalk and locked the doors. If I wanted this treatment, I said into the window, I could have stayed in Detroit, where UAW security had a standing order to keep me from entering the premises. Standing here in rural Alabama, I wondered if that order was worldwide. Maybe my photograph was hanging in every union boss's office.

There was a discount cigarette outlet next to the UAW shack. A good ol' boy sauntered out in a Crimson Tide ball cap, sagging blue jeans, and a wiry beard that tapered into his sagging mouth. He asked about the camera. I asked about unions.

He said he knew about the union, all right, having once worked in the steel mills around Birmingham, now long gone. If he ever thought any good of them, the feeling disappeared soon after the unemployment checks stopped coming. The union might have had its purpose way back when, but so did he. Now he didn't count. Now he was just a blip in a monthly economic report, one of the many millions who didn't exist anymore to a government that didn't seem to care. Except for the fact that he was standing right here. Free trade may have made things cheaper, but what's the good of that if you've got no job?

Union, bud? Ha ha, he cackled. They ruined the economy.

It was clear. In America, it was now every man for himself. The free flow of capital across international borders had made a man like him expendable, crippled, grabbing what he could before the plate was taken away. The union was great when it got you a high wage. But the union is your enemy when it blocks your ability to get one of the last good jobs. No company wants to open a factory when they'll have to deal with unions. Or when the union boss is hooking up his nephew instead of you.

Don't lecture the southern workingman in today's America about solidarity, brotherhood, shared sacrifice, or seniority unless you want to make him laugh. They don't ask about seniority when you're applying to mop floors or wipe old people's asses at the retirement home.

How're you eating? I asked him.

Got a freezer full of squirrel.

Squirrel? Goddamn, I thought, had it really come to that? Parboiling rodent on the grill? As he drove off in a beat-up Toyota pickup, I stood there in the parking lot considering this man living somewhere out in the backwoods, prepping for Armageddon with a freezer stuffed with squirrel, a crate full of ammo, and a carton of no-brand cigarettes. He wasn't praying for the Rapture. He was praying for a couple frozen turkeys to fall off the back of a delivery truck.

A man in the Deep South hoarding squirrel in a deep freezer. *Jesus H. Christ.* But people were going hungry and a man had to do what he had to do to eat. It wasn't only in the South. It was no different in the North in my hometown.

A man fishing from a pier sees a leg. Then a second. Then a third. Legs don't come in threes; he knows that much about anatomy. Random bits of dead people bobbing along the banks of the Detroit River. White people bits. There's a sheet billowing in the current like the sail of a schooner. There is also a suitcase and a Skil Saw visible below the waterline.

The fisherman calls the police.

The TV guy arrives too.

*Hey! I know you!* the anglers shout. TV reporters are the closest thing to celebrities in flyover country. Selfies are taken. Good tidings are exchanged at low tide. That's when you know you've made it in the shitshow, son. Bobbing bits in the background.

*Say Cheese!*

Homicide dicks eventually arrive. Some stouthearted black men are still fishing from the pier, taking care to cast over the horror. These are those unrehearsed moments. A natural interaction between white cop and black bystander. Them versus Us. The hungry masses versus the Man. *This unscripted reality never makes the news: too complicated, too real.*

*What the fuck are you doing? shouts a detective. This is a crime scene!*

*One fisherman nods toward a pail full of fish.*

*They hitting right now. What you expect me to do?*

# No Color but the
# Red of Blood

DETROIT (SPRING)—

My grandpa's old house on Birwood Street was still for sale, the asking price still around $500. It's been like that for years. I was thinking about my grandfather and the house he built with his own hands on the West Side of Detroit that I always tell myself I'm going to buy and fix up. But I know that's a lie. I'm never going to buy it. The neighborhood is too fucked up. Storefronts boarded up with the roofs falling in. Abandoned house after abandoned house, the window frames long gone, having been scrapped for their aluminum. An occasional drape still hanging.

My grandpa was born black in Baton Rouge and died white in Detroit. He came north and *passed*. I don't judge him. Life and race and class in America are complicated and paradoxical things. But it is easier to be white. Grandpa knew that. We all know that.

I was thinking of Grandpa as I walked around the bombed-out East Side of the city because I was gathering material for a story about a mob that had savaged a man who accidentally hit a child with his truck after the kid stepped into traffic, playing a game of chicken. When the driver stopped to come to the aid of the child in front of a gas station, he was savagely attacked.

The story was all over town. All over the country. All over the internet. Fear was spreading exponentially. Electronically. After what happened, I suspect lots of people in Detroit were getting guns. And if they weren't getting guns, I figured, then for sure they weren't stopping for gas. What made this story delicious bait for the masses was that the motorist, Steve Utash, was white. The mob, witnesses said, was made up of a dozen black men. A crowd of on-lookers gathered while the group beat Utash within an inch of his life. He was saved by Deborah Hughes, a black woman and retired nurse who carried a .38 in her purse.

I had tracked down Hughes through a friend. She was hiding in her own apartment, afraid to come out. She lived in a two-level apartment complex that looked as though it once functioned as a motel. There were bars on the windows and door. Hughes told me that on the day Utash was attacked, she saw the violent crowd from her bedroom, grabbed her gun, and, at great risk to her life, jumped through the mob. After attending to the child, who wasn't critically injured, she lay across the body of Mr. Utash and promised that she would put a bullet through the next person to strike him.

It don't matter to me your color, she said of the incident. We all bleed red.

Eventually, four adult men were convicted of assault to do great bodily harm less than murder and a juvenile was convicted on an assault charge with intent to murder; an ethnic intimidation charge was dropped. Utash, nearly unrecognizable from the beating, spent nine days in a coma but lived.

Was the beating race-related? Probably. This is America, after all. This is Detroit. We have a history. The city has endured three major race riots. In my lifetime, I remember two out-of-work white autoworkers angry about Japanese inroads into the U.S. auto industry beating a Chinese American man to death in 1982 because they thought he was Japanese. In the early 1990s, white cops went to prison for beating a black motorist to death. The year before, a white man shot a black woman to death after her car broke down and she was wandering the neighborhood, presumably looking for help. Now this, I thought. So the circle spins on. Black mob. White fear. More guns.

You're a brave man to be here, said an older Arab man standing in front of a store with bars on its windows catty-corner from Hughes's apartment block, which was across the street from the gas station where Utash's beating took place. I saw them beat the man, he told me. Disgusting. They rob, they steal, they don't care about nothing. Don't stay around here too long, he warned.

There it was, the ubiquitous *They.*

*They* rob my store. *They* steal my tires. *They* keep their boot on my neck.

It was just rage, a young black man explained to me at the liquor store that completed the geographic square of dysfunction. Rage. There's just this feeling that *they* keep us down. *They* won't let us live.

There it was again. *They. They* keep us down. *They* won't let us live. What rage was he talking about? What was so different now that *They* hadn't been through before? *Them.* What could *We* do for *Them?*

When in America, I wondered, would it be about *Us?*

Sadly, the talk after the attack on Utash wasn't about *Us*. It wasn't about a man who stopped to do the right thing. It wasn't about Hughes, the gun-toting angel of mercy who saw no color except the red of blood. It wasn't about the use of justifiable force or the value of carrying a sidearm. It wasn't about that at all. It was about *They*.

White people asked: Where were *They*, those old-school civil rights advocates who usually spoke out against such beatings? Where was Reverend Al? Why did it take Jesse Jackson almost two weeks to say something? Not that any of those white people really wanted famous civil rights leaders coming to town and marching around, shouting Hey-Hey, Ho-Ho! What they seemed to be demanding was an admission from black leaders that blacks harbor racial hatred too.

But leaders nationally and in Detroit specifically stayed curiously silent. A medical fund was established for Utash, but it took more than a week to convene a vigil for him as he lay in a coma. Until that moment, not even Mike Duggan—the first elected white mayor of Detroit in forty years—had made a public appearance addressing the incident (though he did put out a weak press release and a tweet). Nor had any city council member. And nothing from President Obama. Rage and hopelessness were no excuses here. All Detroit, whether black or white, noticed the silence.

Three black men I spoke with at the gas station acknowledged this two-way street. They called Utash an honorable man for stopping to help when too many people in this city don't. They mocked the silence of civic leaders. They wanted to know why the mayor had not come to their neighborhood. They knew the score. They were Americans. And they also knew that we couldn't expect those leaders to solve this riddle of ours called race.

The fact is, it's hard to be white in America too, especially if you're struggling in a struggling place like Detroit. You do the best you can. Just ask Utash, who lay in a hospital bed.

A fund-raiser was put together for Utash's medical bills. His son was at the event, held at a local bar, collecting cash and well-wishes for his father. Afterward, the son went to a strip joint on 8-Mile with an Egyptian theme. According to what the police and strippers later told me, Junior had himself a wild night at the emporium. It ended with Junior calling the cops, complaining that one of the dancers had stolen $1,500 from him. When asked about the source of the money, the son cried, but insisted he had exaggerated the amount stolen. It was really just four hundred bucks, he claimed, money from his unemployment check and most definitely not money from his father's fund-raiser.

Maybe. Who knows? Life is sordid and complicated and money doesn't just step off a curb. Besides, you know how *Those* kind of people are.

In the meantime, I called friends, trying to find Deborah Hughes a new place to live. She was all that stood between freedom and prison for a handful of thugs. Someone was bound to kill her. But she refused to move away. It's principle, she said. *They're* not gonna run me out of my own home.

*They.*

The day Utash was beaten, another pocket of rage erupted in America. This one out west. This time it was white people and *They* had guns. Things were moving fast and so were we.

# The White Man's Last Stand

Sunrise came over the desert, and a feeling of complete and utter weirdness hung with it. Was it the bum weed we'd scored the night before outside a spiritless whorehouse in the cold desert mountains? I was convinced it was laced with Ajax or bathroom incense. My nose was burning and my innards were rumbling and there wasn't a tree or a port-o-john in sight as we rolled past a platoon of obese revolutionaries parked along the shoulder of the bridge spanning the Virgin River. They were sitting in lawn chairs, their RVs festooned with flags and signage decrying Waco, Ruby Ridge, the Alamo!

Maybe it was the sniper at the top of the ridge that gave me the jitters, watching with binoculars from a foxhole fortified with sandstone, the barrel of his long arm glinting in the sun. We drove across the bridge, and there was another sentinel, an intimidating guy with a mustache and assault rifle, dressed in an olive jumpsuit, flak jacket, and beret, blocking the access road to Cliven Bundy's complex.

There wasn't a badge in sight, since all the cops and federal agents and sheriff's deputies had been run off a few days earlier by armed militiamen and ranchers on horseback, cheered on by the bored suburbanites who had come out to watch the good old-fashioned range war and were now having a breakfast of Doritos with ranch dressing on the side of the road. *¡Viva la revolución! And this new no-drip spout on the ranch is a marvel of human ingenuity too!*

We had a few hours to kill before our semi-sorta-arranged meeting with Bundy, the leader of this whole deal, who had been at war with the federal government for twenty years over his self-proclaimed right to graze his livestock on public lands for free and had now decided to bring it to a head. Better not to fuck with this guy in the beret, I thought. Instead, we decided to pull into a militia camp near the fork in the road to the Bundy ranch and wait for the call.

Play it cool, I told my cameraman Bob, who was wearing an American flag bandanna to protect his bald, speckled head against the sun. Move too fast and someone might get the wrong idea, mistake us for feds, narcs, friends of the court. Bob also likes guns very much and gets overly excited when he's in proximity to them. Mix that with a bunk weed hangover, and I figured it was better to take it nice and slow for everybody's sake. I leaned against the quarter panel and lit my cigarette. That's when I heard the familiar western drawl.

Goddamn! I'll be goddamned! Charlie, is that you?

I'll be goddamned. It was Lil Dog. He was unmistakable: pot-bellied, silver-bearded, bare-chested, with boots, khaki shorts, and slouch hat. An Army veteran and retired fisherman. At sixty-five years old, he was a rumbling, sloshing vat of chaos and conspiracies, a citizen-soldier of numerous domestic campaigns against government tyranny, federal overreach, border intrusion, and the general spiritual pussification of the American man. He had founded a militia based in the Southwest known as the Mountain Minutemen, and I'd met him about eight years earlier, when I was a newspaper reporter—the first time he'd made a national spectacle of himself.

Back then, he was standing sentry on the California–Mexico border and had plopped himself on a hill directly in a cartel smuggling route, even though nobody had asked him to. He had fancied himself a twenty-four-hours-a-day, seven-days-a-week "scout." He flew a large American flag from a makeshift thirty-foot pole, carried a .45 in his waistband, and lived in relative luxury in an RV with a toilet. I wrote a newspaper story about him and his war—not with illegal immigrants, none of whom he ever seemed to apprehend, but with Patch, a one-eyed Vietnam vet keeping vigil on the next hill over.

War often has its root in the most inane and inconsequential of incidents. These two men, once friends and residents of the same hill, broke into war over the well-being of a puppy. The misunderstanding devolved into words. Then insults. Patch moved to another hill. Lil Dog baited him as a phony war hero, comparing him to male genitalia and rifling off an email message to CNN calling him a swine who lived in a cat box. This led to fisticuffs on the main street of the border town, when the men happened to come off their hilltops at the same time for water and supplies. Patch, a vigorous, leathery specimen of a man, gave Lil Dog four chances to take back the insults, which Lil Dog refused to do, resulting in the breakage of Lil Dog's eyeglasses.

Since then, Lil Dog had kept himself in the news, narrating a grainy "snuff" film of himself shooting dead a migrant who was illegally traversing the border. "This video shows how to keep a Home Depot parking lot empty," he wrote to sympathizers in an email. Under withering pressure from the internet and law enforcement, Lil Dog admitted the video was a fake, that it was he himself acting as the murdered migrant.

And so here he was again at the latest media spectacle. He wasn't doing much at the minute, he admitted. Throughout his life, there'd been a couple of tax liens, a string of petty controversies in previous judicial jurisdictions, but he was living now, he said, with a new old lady—a Mexican American no less—in a walled-in neighborhood somewhere near Vegas.

Lil Dog told me he came charging up Interstate 15 a few days earlier, after he'd seen one of Bundy's sons get Tasered on cable TV. By that time, the old man's compound had been surrounded by armed federal agents, who began confiscating the family cattle at gunpoint.

Bundy had been making the novel argument that the federal government had no jurisdiction over the federal land he'd been squatting on for the past two decades to feed and water his cattle. His argument was twofold: He had ancestral rights to use the land dating back to his grandfather, and he, Bundy, was a sovereign citizen of the Great State of Nevada, but not the United States of America, and the land belonged to Nevada. By that reckoning, there could be no way he owed the government $1 million.

The federal Bureau of Land Management saw it differently. It argued Bundy was a fraud, a mooch, a deadbeat who'd made millions from livestock sales while the rest of us paid taxes to improve the land he used. The federal courts agreed with the federal government, quite naturally. And so federal agents came in force to garnish Bundy's livestock. That's when a few-hundred-strong army of private citizens arrived with their long arms, stood the government down, and freed the cattle.

Tyranny! Lil Dog shouted shrilly, the voice of a half dozen Lil Dogs echoing off the valley walls in agreement. They have no right to take the man's cattle, he declared. Tyranny!

Well, it is the public's land, I reminded him. Mine, yours, ours. Somebody's got to pay to keep the land in order. Why do I have to pay for Bundy?

That launched Lil Dog into a litany of complaints: unemployment, homeless veterans scrounging through garbage pails in the alleys of the big cities, welfare for illegal immigrants and their children, cash distributions to foreign countries. We're not giving a shit about people in our own country, he barked. It's a travesty!

What all this had to do with scofflaw cows, I couldn't say. But bovinity notwithstanding, you would know what Lil Dog was trying to get at if you'd been anywhere in America over the past decade besides the Hollywood Hills, Manhattan, or D.C. People were put out. Put out of their houses. Put out of their jobs. Put out on their asses. Losing ground. A good lot of them were veterans, many recently returned from tours in Iraq or Afghanistan, or both. Men and women who had gone off to war while the well-heeled of the nation went to the shopping mall. And they returned to a nation divided. Now they were living in crappy suburban apartments somewhere, their prospects bleak, wondering where their piece of the American pie had gone. What had they fought for? Rage became the companion of confusion. Like the kid in the ghetto of Detroit: rage.

And who speaks to the veterans' frustrations? Who appreciates their service? The empty trope of "thank you for your service" means 10 percent off at Arby's and the honor of being the first to get on a plane. No one's hiring. Too many are strung out and they're taking their own lives. Thank you for your service.

Most soldiers take it stoically and get on with the business of living. But others turn on the television and damn! There's a guy who gets it! There's a man with answers! Water rights? Grazing allotments? I'm driving an Uber, but this sounds like tyranny to me! Forward ho! To the Bundy compound!

Lil Dog was now drawing a pretty good crowd. Our camera was like an enema for a constipated frustration. The boys and I set up a soapbox, wrapped the microphone in an American flag, and invited public comment. The patriots came like flies to a cowhide. One unemployed Army vet from Phoenix got up to say he was there in the name of the individual's liberties, as enshrined in the Bill of Rights. Pressed to enumerate those rights, he stumbled a bit.

Okay, he said haltingly, wait a minute. Right to free speech (shoot your mouth) and the right to bear arms (shoot your gun). Thou shall not . . . Oh, wait a minute . . . Sorry, yeah, I'm drawing a blank here.

Sprinkle that in with a catalog of gripes ranging from Obamacare to the desert tortoise, illegals bum-rushing the border to the cost of gasoline, fiat currency, the Chinese plan to colonize Mars, and you pretty much get the picture.

Lil Dog invited us under his canopy for a Dr Pepper. Somebody had lunch cooking in a skillet. Beans and bacon. In a skillet. This is really too goddamned much, I told Lil Dog. It's like a fucking Mel Brooks movie, except you're all armed.

And we'll fucking use them if we gotta, he proclaimed. Fucking feds come over that hill with their weapons, and see if I'm kidding. Hahahahaha!

He pointed out a portable outhouse, and I went to avail myself of it. It hadn't been cleaned out and was near overflowing like a gigantic overstuffed pastry bag. Ah! These must be the sights and smells of liberty, I thought to myself. Apparently, toilet attendants don't show up for work during the revolution.

Returning to Lil Dog's camp, I was thinking it was time to break camp before something went wrong. Passions were running high and I told Lil Dog we were just going to take our chances and head up to Old Man Bundy's compound, phone call or no.

We're just going to drive right on past that sniper guy in the beret and sunglasses over there, I said. Do you know him? You don't? Just if something goes wrong, you understand?

I promised Lil Dog we would be back later with some beer and booze, but it was a promise I had no intention of keeping. The only thing that gives Bob a bigger boner than firearms is firewater. Put them together and you have a very volatile situation, hombre. I wasn't looking to instigate an unintentional fiasco of violence here in the High Kingdom of Cliven. Better to just drive way. Nice and slow.

We pulled out of the militia camp, took a hard left, and kicked up a cloud of dust that billowed over the sniper in sunglasses. He didn't move, didn't motion us to stop. Unlike the paid goon at the Mercedes plant down in Alabama, this old boy seemed to understand that the public has a right to public roads, God bless him. Liberty!

It was a beautiful country of scrub oak and sage and dark red soil. As the road buckled and dipped, the valley opened up for a moment and we could see the rippling Virgin River, the only natural-looking tributary I'd ever seen in this part of Nevada. A Bundy cow and a calf were watering at the bank, others grazing on the grass along the tributary. A few days earlier, these same cows had been captives of the U.S. government. Now the cowboys were betting they'd won. It wasn't a wager I was willing to make.

Nevada senator Harry Reid had gone on TV calling Bundy and his supporters domestic terrorists. And when Harry calls you out, you know you've got trouble. Reid, the Senate minority leader, was the most powerful man in Nevada, if not the country. The guy ran the Mob out of Vegas when he was head of the Nevada Gaming Commission, for heaven's sake, and if Harry wants your cows off the river, dagnabit, your cows are going to be off that river, come hell or high water.

Water is power in the West. Water is the wellspring of money. And money is the wellspring of politics. Water is necessary to lubricate the gargantuan casinos of Las Vegas, just as it's necessary for the gigantic development being built just twenty miles west of the Virgin River, a forty-three-thousand-acre city of the future with golf courses and swimming pools in the deepest bowels of the desert. Ironically, the development was on temporary mothballs as the power broker behind it was preparing to make his new home in the federal penitentiary for illegally funneling campaign money to . . . Senate Minority Leader Harry Reid, himself the son of a failed gold miner.

Maybe this whole range war was about water, maybe it was about gold, maybe it was just the government wanting its money. But it wasn't lost on many in the area that the man charged with running Bundy off the river, the director of the federal Bureau of Land Management, was a thirty-seven-year-old snot nose named Neil Kornze who had once been a gofer in the Senate office of . . . Harry Reid.

So it was easy to see why Harry wasn't much appreciated in these parts.

When we arrived at the Bundy ranch, we were stopped at the main gate by another man, shaped like a bowling ball decorated in bad tattoos, a Kevlar vest, a holstered sidearm, one-way shades, and a checkered scarf, the kind favored by Osama bin Laden and Yasser Arafat. It was a little accoutrement picked up during his tours in the Middle East, the sentry said.

Yes, yes. I've been there, I told him. It's called a keffiyeh. Very useful in the heat and sand.

Anyway, you can't be too careful out here, the sentry counseled. If the elements don't get you, the snipers will. The feds sent drones. The BLM killed some cattle. There's no telling where they'll stop. No telling who's a snitch.

Not wanting to be taken for a rat, I showed him my bupkis press badge. Says it right there: NEWS MEDIA PRESS OFFICIAL IDENTIFICATION.

Satisfied, he radioed down to the ranch. *It's Buddha,* he spat into the walkie-talkie. *We got some media up here. Over.*

Buddha, huh? Is that how you write it on your tax forms?

It's BOOD-*a.* No "h."

What do you do for a living, bro? I asked.

A crackle returned from the radio. A disembodied voice: *Booda, come on. Over.*

Booda tells me he's a United States Marine. A special forces sniper and former mercenary for the Blackwater contracting company. Then, into the radio: *You got Booda. Over.* Booda says he did tours in Iraq and Afghanistan.

*You say you got media up there? Over.*

Booda says he took an oath to defend the United States Constitu-

tion, and that's what he's doing here: protecting the man who is leading a well-regulated militia to battle a tyrannical government.

I didn't know the Marine Corps gave leave for that sort of thing,
I said.

*Yeah, we got media up here,* he replied to the radio. *They say they
got an appointment. Over.*

Then Booda said to me: I can't give you any more detail than
that, you understand? Classified. Heavy stuff, see what I'm getting
at? Crazy as hell over there. I can tell you that.

*Okay,* the voice came back over the radio, *go ahead and escort
them down. The boss is just finishing up with some people. Taking a
few selfies. Over.*

*Roger that,* Booda replied before leading us on.

B undy's home was nice and well kept, small and unassuming,
made smaller still by the gaggle of hangers-on buzzing in his or-
bit. There was the wagon wheel entrance, potted plants hanging near
the door, flowers standing in the window, a horseshoe, a wood carving
of a mustachioed cowboy, all made dreamlike by the flesh-and-blood
buckaroo leaning against a timber joist. Bundy was tall and potbel-
lied and, unlike his security squadron, carried an air of hospitality.

I follow all the laws of Nevada, Bundy explained to me after
shaking hands, but I don't even recognize the United States government as existing.

That's an interesting point of view, sir, I responded, considering
those American and Marine Corps flags tacked to that post there.
The Supreme Court has ruled that these are federal lands and
you're trespassing. That's the law. That's the state law. That's the
federal law. Their authorities are vested by the Constitution.

Mebbe. But I'm a-saying that I have ancestral claims to this land. My grandfather worked these lands.

I reminded him that the red man was living here long before the white man, long before his granddaddy, and that his granddaddy was able to take the land in the first place with the aid and abettal of the United States government.

Well, I think I was treated even worse than the Indian, Bundy said. The federal government has treated me with force and cruelty.

And there was the rub. A government that once assisted the white man was now turning on the white man's grandson. Now that there was something the government wanted from him, it was treating him like an Indian, at least in Bundy's mind, running him off his rightful place. And when that happens, well, men like him don't recognize the government as legitimate anymore. Conspiracies baked in half-truths tend to balloon like bread dough. Cherry-picked passages of the Constitution are recited with a reverence reserved for psalms.

The fact that Bundy was claiming ancestral rights was, not surprisingly, stirring up feelings among the Indian peoples in these parts. Treaties are part of the supreme law of the land, and treaties between the United States and Indian people have long been violated and outright ignored. The Shoshone hold claim to two-thirds of Nevada, and if the government was going to enforce its own laws, not only would it have to vacate, but so would men like Bundy.

That is a legitimate question, Bundy agreed. He might consider giving it back to the Indians, but he vowed that he sure as heck wasn't going to submit to the United States government.

I told him I knew some Indians who would be willing to help him pack up his belongings. In fact, the whole tribe could be here within the hour with a U-Haul. Bundy's armed sycophants soughed through their noses. Booda, he of the classified war stories, was standing next to a guy in an ill-fitting Stetson filming us filming. It seemed like a bad omen. There was something unnerving about these hangers-on, something celluloid about the straw hats, something store-bought in their tattoos, masking perhaps a lack of real scars, authentic and earned.

Bundy had his beef, that was true enough, however shifting and spurious his arguments may have been. And his followers had succeeded in running the federal government off federal land. But Uncle Sam would be back, whether it be a week, a month, a year, or a century. The government takes what the government desires, ancestral rights or no. Just ask the modern-day Geronimo eking it out four hundred miles away in a high-desert valley of the Cortez Range.

# How Green Was the Red Woman's Valley

The thunder grew louder. Everything rumbling. A dust cloud billowed off the asphalt road that split the valley. Semi-trucks loaded with slag stampeded across the basin like an ancient herd. And then all went quiet. Only the sound of rain softly pelting the aluminum roof could be heard, forlorn.

It was all gone, the cattle, the horses. The livestock posts planted a decade ago had been ripped from the earth. The pickup truck now a rusting carcass. The apple trees were withered old bones. The windows on the homestead were aged and dirty. Inside, the table still set for supper. A spoon. A plate. A salt shaker. Unwashed dishes in the sink. Cornmeal in the cupboard. A blanket on the old yellow mattress. The damned death rattle of rain on the roof.

They killed us, the old Indian woman said, considering some old mail left on the countertop. Land is life.

I had met Carrie Dann ten years earlier during her range war with the U.S. government, and I had liked her very much. We set fencing poles and stretched barbed wire for her livestock. We ate wild rabbit stew with Wonder Bread and margarine. One evening, as the desert air began to cool and the grasshoppers came to life, she told me then that as far as indigenous people go, without the land the Shoshone people would cease to be.

She was near eighty now. Old but sturdy, five feet tall, gray hair, lined face, knotty hands hanging from a dirty canvas jacket. She had abandoned this eight-hundred-acre homestead a few years back after her sister Mary died in a ranching accident, heartbroken and unable to manage it alone. Her brother Clifford was of no use anymore. Unable to see or hear, he spent his days sitting in front of a television back in the village, near the county road that glittered with broken beer bottles.

Like Cliven Bundy, the Dann clan fought the federal government for decades over the right to freely graze their livestock on what the government claimed was public land. And like Bundy, the Danns claimed ancestral rights, the difference being that the Shoshone people had been there for a thousand years and their ancestral rights were prescribed in the Treaty of Ruby Valley. The treaty bequeathed eighty million acres to the tribe, about two-thirds of modern-day Nevada, plus parts of Utah and the watershed that provides the tap water to Southern California.

The agreement granted white settlers passage through Shoshone lands across the Great Basin—but no rights to settle it. Purely a peace and friendship deal. But the colonists and the government took the land anyway, and all the gold and silver and water beneath it.

In the late 1970s, a panel of federal bureaucrats acknowledged the treaty, but, citing a novel concept called "gradual encroachment," they ruled that Nevada no longer belonged to the Shoshone and hadn't since 1872. They awarded the tribe a settlement of fifteen cents an acre, an amount based on the land's 1872 value.

The tribe refused the money, so the federal government accepted $26 million on the Shoshone's behalf and put it in the bank to collect interest. The Danns fought this arrangement all the way to the Supreme Court, which ruled that since the federal government had accepted the money from the federal government on the Indians' behalf, that constituted a settlement with the tribes, and thus the treaty was null and void.

Get off the land, red woman.

The Danns fought on. Not with guns, but with matchsticks and gasoline and sit-ins. Clifford was sent to prison for trying to light himself on fire. The elderly sisters tried to hide their horses in the back range, but federal agents swooped in with helicopters and assault rifles and cattle trucks. The livestock was taken away and auctioned to satisfy the Danns' $5 million fine for unlawfully grazing on their ancestral lands.

No paramilitary came to help the Indians. No militia. No Booda. No white man in a fifth wheel. No cable TV reporters dressed in earth tones. Everyone's got love for the indigenous peoples of America and their plight, until it comes time to pay up. That's when the red romance gives way to the white realities of power. Bundy, remember, said he would consider handing his land back to the Indian, but he never actually did.

I guess we just weren't sexy enough. The old woman cackled. Two old indigenous ladies. I'm not all that pretty, and I'm not white at all. But, you know, we're not violent people anyway. You're not supposed to take any life unless you're gonna eat it. Oh well.

The Bureau of Land Management claimed the Dann sisters

were destroying life on the range. Overgrazing it. Putting the natural order in jeopardy. One wonders if this was truly the reason for running them off, because just a few weeks after the Danns' livestock was confiscated, one of the continent's largest gold mines opened in the valley, near where the road elbows east and the asphalt becomes gravel. This mine uses cyanide and groundwater to separate gold particles from rock. The process is done in a gigantic open pit. The mine was owned by Barrick Gold, a powerful behemoth with financial and familial ties to . . . Senator Harry Reid.

Looking out now above Carrie Dann's shoulder, to the west, where the sun was orange and fading, I could make out the peak of a foothill that had been sawed away by the gold miners. Dust rose from the grinding of the semi-trucks.

They fucked you, I said.

No, she corrected. They raped me.

It was an important distinction. Fucking implies you asked for it.

Months later, Cliven Bundy would be arrested in Oregon and charged with a raft of counts, including conspiracy, obstruction, and assault on a federal officer, for his role in the Bunkerville standoff. Booda would be exposed as a poseur and liar, a man whose only real service seems to have been at the self-serve lunch counter.

Clifford Dann would continue to spend his afternoons watching cartoons he could not see. And Carrie Dann, destitute and broken, would move into a drafty house behind an imposing wooden fence, just up the road from the gold mine.

And Harry? Well, Senator Reid, the country boy from a Nevada dirt patch called Searchlight, would sell his old family homestead and its fourteen ghost mines to another gold company for $1.7 million. And after fifty years as a public servant, he would step down from the U.S. Senate, move to Las Vegas, and retire a very wealthy man.

Harry wouldn't talk to us. He wouldn't return our calls. We were barred from his office in the Federal Building. His new Vegas address was unlisted. We had no time to wait for his Eminence to emerge from his upscale tortoise hole. The Texas border was being besieged by the poor and huddled masses yearning to be free.

*NAFTA means jobs. American jobs. If I didn't believe that, I wouldn't support this agreement.*

—FORMER U.S. PRESIDENT BILL CLINTON

*The real end winner of NAFTA is going to be Mexico because we have the human capital. We have that resource that is vital to the success of the U.S. economy.*

—FORMER MEXICAN PRESIDENT VICENTE FOX

*Our nation has lost one-third of its manufacturing jobs since NAFTA, a deal signed by Bill Clinton and supported strongly by Hillary Clinton. And by the way, the single worst trade deal ever made in history anywhere.*

—DONALD TRUMP

*NAFTA, supported by the secretary [Hillary Clinton], cost us 800,000 jobs nationwide, tens of thousands of jobs in the Midwest. Permanent normal trade relations with China cost us millions of jobs. Look, I was on a picket line in the early 1990s against NAFTA because you didn't need a PhD in economics to understand that American workers should not be forced to compete against people in Mexico making 25 cents an hour.*

—SENATOR BERNIE SANDERS

*Here's a stark fact: During America's last two decades, five million manufacturing jobs were lost. Part of this was due to the machine. That is, people were replaced by robots and computers. In economic lingo, this means that those who still had a job became "more productive" as output and profits increased per worker. But the workers did not share in this rise of productivity. Their wages remained stagnant while CEOs' compensation tripled to more than three hundred times the average worker's wage, and many times the company was able to dodge federal taxes altogether.*

*And then there were the intentional job losses from the global trade deals that had sent American jobs to the Third World or allowed the Third World preferential access to American markets— three-quarters of a million jobs to Mexico, at least another two million to China, and so on.*

*Now that the real estate bubble had popped, working-class Americans were competing with Latino laborers for the menial work. White and black men, I could see across the country by the gardening trucks, had returned to the lawn mower.*

*Some experts argue that free flow of capital and people has benefited American consumers with cheaper goods. As true as that is, think about it for a moment. That's like letting a thousand foreign meat cutters through the door, then telling the local butcher he'll benefit from cheaper ham.*

*Remember all the cheery chatter from politicians about these free-trade agreements? American workers do. We were going to get rich. The Mexicans were going to get rich, and the flood of illegal immigration was going to evaporate to a trickle.*

*Except none of that happened.*

# A Sea of Brown

Identification, please.

It was the Texas Rangers this time. Or Park Police. Whoever, but I was starting to notice a pattern here. A nation leery of itself becomes a police state. But a badge is a badge. America, secure and suspicious. Love it or leave it.

Yes sir. Here you go: NEWS MEDIA PRESS OFFICIAL IDEN-TIFICATION.

Who gave you permission to come out here? He was wearing The Glasses, you know, the one-ways, like Booda wore.

A rancher had given me permission to check out his property. Ever since the federal government built an eighteen-foot wall to the north of his spread to prevent flooding and illegal immigrants from running through town, the rancher's Texas plot had been walled off from the rest of the United States. He'd been living in no-man's-land, caught between Mexico and Texas. It was still technically American territory, but because the border wall was a mile north, and he was existing now in a gray land, a purgatory of the shadows.

Cops didn't bother patrolling this forgotten, vestigial piece of America, and eventually, narco-traffickers ran the rancher off with guns. Smugglers ransacked his house. Migrant women and children from Central America now used it as a resting point, their used diapers and toiletries discarded beneath the mesquite tree. But I wasn't telling the cop this.

Are you filming me?

Yes sir.

Stop filming, he demanded.

No sir. First Amendment. Sorry.

You've got one minute to get off this road.

Or what?

Or you're subject to arrest.

On what grounds?

Trespassing.

Trespassing?

Yes sir.

A hundred thousand women and children were suddenly flooding into the United States, many of them walking up the very road we were standing on. They would immediately surrender to the American authorities, knowing that because of a loophole in the law, they couldn't be deported. At least not the unattended children, who accounted for half the traffic. The other half? The adult women? The authorities processed them too, and seventy-two hours later, everybody had an immigration court date and a bus ticket to a city of their choice. According to Congress, more than 90 percent of them would never show up for court.

You're going to arrest me for trespassing? An American citizen? That's ironic, Officer.

You now have thirty seconds, sir.

More cruisers pulled up. Border Patrol. State Park police. The whole enchilada. We were only a couple months into *The Americans,* but one thing had become real obvious: Lots of people in this country have a gun, claiming a little piece of authority. Those who have none officially behave as thugs, jackboots, obstructionists.

But this was different. Now I had an official Law Man running me off a public road because Texas was being invaded by a horde of mamas and papooses.

The United States had spent more than a trillion dollars since 9/11 to secure its borders, and we couldn't handle a wave of nursery school children. It was a national humiliation, and they were taking it out on the reporters.

Fifteen seconds.

I lit a cigarette. That countdown trick doesn't even work on ten-year-olds. The ranger returned to his cruiser. I made a fake phone call. He wasn't going to arrest us, but he sure as hell wasn't going to let us down to the Rio Grande to get a photo of some kids surrendering to authorities.

All right, guys, pack it in, I told Bob and Matt, who were relishing the attention because Matt knew it was good TV and Bob is a psycho when it comes to the Man. We'll try the state park a couple miles upriver.


They fucking ran you out of there?

The question came from Albert Spratte, a big, salt-and-pepper buzz-cut white guy, again with the one-way glasses. Spratte was a lifelong Border Patrol agent and was so upset that a lifetime of work had devolved into chasing toddlers around that he'd agreed to meet us on his day off in muggy ninety-five-degree heat.

Man, that can't even be legal, he said. The government just doesn't want you to see how bad it is, what a failure this is.

I'd heard it more times than I could remember from Border Patrol agents. I'd heard it in Arizona, Washington State, California, Michigan. The border is a failure. Most of those telling me this were Latino agents, upset at the crime and drugs and the jumping ahead of those trying to gain legitimate entry into the United States. I'd heard it from a crew in Laredo, Texas, as they were inspecting a drainpipe, filled with shoes and clothes, that illegal immigrants had used to bypass the border fence.

Bro, one of the agents said then, don't put my name on this, but if the people really knew what was going on, they'd flip the fuck out.

We were talking with Spratte in Anzalduas Park, a nice cool place located at a bend in the Rio Grande in McAllen. There were barbecue pits and shade trees, the current made slow by a dam in the river. There were also dozens of law enforcement types from every jurisdiction, since this was where TV went to get pictures of migrant hopefuls being smuggled in on Jet Skis, Spratte told me.

Jet Skis! The ingenuity of these smugglers. The ability to cope, to change with the times. Years earlier, for a newspaper story, I had attempted to sneak back into the United States with the help of a coyote, or smuggler. I'd taken a taxi out into the Mexican desert, where the meeting point was. When I walked down the ravine and parted the reeds, I found three hundred people divided into groups of fifty and one hundred, ready to embark on the very dangerous three-day journey across the unknown and inhospitable desert floor. A human cattle drive. Their eyes, reflected in the night, widened in fright at the sight of a gringo coming upon them. Now you could do it by a twenty-second sleigh ride across the Rio! *¡Que fantástico!*

On the Mexican side, there was a sandy beach where women and children played. A hundred yards from them were camped about two dozen tough-looking guys with Jet Skis, trailers, pickup trucks with windows tinted black, and coolers of beer.

I stepped into the bush, blew up a rubber kayak I had brought for the trip, and slipped on a straw hat and a red-white-and-blue Speedo with "USA" stamped across the ass. A *güero* like myself flailing around in a ridiculous costume with a giant yellow banana had two purposes: It would get the attention of the smugglers, and it would make for good TV.

And it worked well. Too well. As I paddled around the Rio Grande, smack dab in the center of the smuggling thoroughfare, chatting with families of sunbathers, the men on the Jet Skis started buzzing me, coming close, making swells in the water. My yellow banana bobbed and weaved. I waved. One hombre on a Jet Ski let off the throttle, smiled at me, then made a throat-cutting gesture with his fingers.

What was remarkable was the lack of cooperation from the Mexican authorities. There were no police or border agents on their side. Dope and human trafficking going on in plain sight, international media in a lather, me padding around in patriotic beachwear, and not a *federale* in sight.

What's more, when U.S. Border Patrol agents apprehend people coming from Mexican territory, the Mexicans will repatriate their own people but not foreign nationals from other countries. And what's even more, when a child arrives alone on American soil, she is entitled by American law to safekeeping and due process to prevent her from being trafficked. But if she arrives with her mother, both can be deported home immediately.

U.S. Representative Henry Cuellar, a sensible law-and-order Democrat from the Texas border town of Laredo, wondered why we weren't putting the Central American families on an immediate flight home, or pushing Mexico harder to do its fair share.

TV pictures of a dozen families returning to Guatemala from America after they'd sold everything they possessed to get to the United States would do more to stop the tidal wave of humanity than anything Congress might cook up, Cuellar had told me the previous day at a hastily convened press conference in a McAllen municipal office building. True immigration reform would take a decade anyhow.

The first lady of Honduras had also attended the presser, where coffee and doughnuts were laid out for the media. The *primera dama* pleaded for more aid to help the poor and famished of her nation, more American-funded programs to help *los niños pobres*. It broke her heart to see children being held in the squalor of American detention cells. They are only looking for a better life, she said. What we need to end this calamity is money, American money. And compassion—yes, this is what is needed.

The first lady dabbed at her eyes on her plump, well-fed face, took a few questions, and left. She did not, however, bother to take any of her *paisanos* back home with her on the presidential jet. I stuffed the leftover doughnuts into my shoulder bag.

Why were the women and children coming now? Simple. President Obama, frustrated with a lack of action in Washington on immigration, had signed an executive order allowing people who were brought illegally to the United States by their parents before the age of sixteen to stay indefinitely. By the time news made it down to

Guatemala, Honduras, and El Salvador, it was understood that Obama was granting mass amnesty to any child and parent who could get to America. That's what the migrants were saying to me, anyway.

That's what a sweet eleven-year-old boy named Domingo from Guatemala told me at the McAllen bus station. After three days in the overcrowded detention center, he and his mother had two tickets to Los Angeles, where they had family, and a far-off date in immigration court.

Domingo was scared, and who could blame the boy? He and his mother had been brought through Mexico by violent smugglers for $5,000. When Domingo walked too slowly for the coyotes, they would cuff his ears. When he got scared at the river and ran off, they hunted him down and beat him. Now there were cameras at the bus station, and protesters on TV.

Do you think life will be better in Los Angeles? he asked me.

Yes, I think so. They have good schools there. And nice things to eat.

It has streets that are very big, no?

Very.

I hope it is good.

It will be. You will see.

I gave the boy twenty dollars and told him not to tell his mother about it. Buy yourself some ice cream when you get to Los Angeles. Study hard and do not be one of those bad boys who grow up to be bad men. I told him to remember his mother's sacrifice, and I welcomed him to America. Sometime in his life, I hope, he will think back on me, that unknown man who encouraged him at a hard moment in his life, and pass it along to the next boy or girl. I gave him one of the press conference doughnuts. Chocolate cream filling.

*Gracias, señor.*

*Claro.*

I headed to the cheerless Mexican consulate in McAllen. It was crowded and smelled of perspiration. The power had gone out. The elevator and air-conditioning were out of order. I was escorted up the fire stairs, seated in a glass-walled lounge, and given coffee in a china cup. I wondered how they kept it warm.

A well-dressed spokesman for the consul general came to see me. I asked him why his government wasn't doing more to stop the flow into the United States from his country.

It is of course a very complicated question, he said. We really cannot speak about the issue at this time. It is . . . how you say? A hot-button issue. Speaking to it may only inflame passions. Are you enjoying your *café*?

Yes, very much, thank you. Would you like a doughnut?

An eighteen-foot concrete wall and hurricane fencing had already been built in McAllen during the Bush-era border security push. It was a bipartisan deal, in 2006. Among the notable Democrats to vote for it: Senators Barack Obama, Hillary Clinton, and Bernie Sanders, the socialist from the hills of Vermont. But the wall doesn't work. To begin with, it was a mile north of the actual border—the Rio Grande—and all a woman or child had to do was make shore and touch a toe to American soil to be granted entry. Sometimes, Spratte told me, they'd sit and wait for hours for the Border Patrol to arrive so they could surrender and be fed and given water.

Every week, the Border Patrol would round up store-bought and makeshift ladders and have them taken off to the dump.

I think there's a guy on that side who makes them, Spratte said. We used to put the ladders in the warehouse, then the warehouse got too full. Now we just throw them away.

Like I said, these coyotes were geniuses. They could work on Wall Street. I still wanted to see these smugglers in action. We left the consulate and the next day we decided to head back to Anzalduas Park to try our luck.

When we arrived, a local constable had detained three Chinese people in new, clean tracksuits who had just made shore by Jet Ski. Chinese in tracksuits! Marvel that. Bob and Matt and I parked the van behind a hedgerow and waited for a Jet Ski to make a break for the American shore. When it did, we jumped out of the van and began rolling. There were two women on the back. One was plainly pregnant. I don't know if it was the cameras, Bob's red-white-and-blue do-rag, or his speckled white legs in white socks, but the coyote freaked out, spun the craft around, and throttled back for Mexico, but not before giving me the finger and shouting, *"Motherfucker! You're costing me money!"* It was my old pal who had buzzed my kayak and threatened to cut my throat earlier.

I smiled and waved.

Spratte came walking up out of nowhere. He was escorting yet another reporter around the park. We were all there. CNN. Breitbart. *Texas Monthly.* BBC. Good God, where was *Field & Stream*? I pointed out the coyote on the opposite side of the river. He lifted the pregnant woman in his arms as though they were newlyweds and set her back on the sand.

Why do I have to do your job, dude? I said to Spratte.

No comment, he grunted. They'll be back once you leave.

. . .

I had no doubt about that. There is an old saying in journalism: When you think you've finished, knock on one more door. With a little resolve, maybe we could actually watch the pregnant woman come ashore and surrender to the Americans. A coyote flipping me off and threatening to sever my jugular is good, but seeing him act as a ferry service while U.S. agents help the woman up the slippery banks would demonstrate the point nicely.

I instructed Matt to take the east side of the bend in the river and Bob the west. I positioned myself in the middle, working as the lookout and attempting to communicate with each of them by hand signals.

The Jet Skis on the Mexican shore fired up, and the smugglers raced in a circular mania, trying to create a distraction. Suddenly, Matt started screaming, but I couldn't make out what he was saying. Maybe he'd been stabbed, I didn't know. I ran to him. He wasn't bleeding at all, but he had found two men lying low in the tall reeds, their legs hidden in the river water. You know the border is out of control when three reporters from Detroit can find illegal immigrants hiding in the mud of a Texas backwater crawling with lawmen.

I couldn't make out their faces in the umbra of the river trees, but I could see that one of them was smiling. A big, dopey grin, wide and toothy. It was weird. They'd been caught smuggling themselves into another country and Twinkles here was as nonchalant as a teenager shoplifting candy. He seemed happy, almost.

I handed them bottles of water.

*Gracias. Gracias, señor.* He gives his name as Ciro.

*¿Cómo viniste?* How'd you come here, Ciro?

*Nadamos.* We swam.

I noticed Ciro and his traveling companion were wearing flip-flops. Think of it: two middle-aged men of average physiology free-styling in Bermuda shorts and sandalwear through an international boundary buzzing with smugglers' Jet Skis and with police boats, the tide running hard and turbid, and neither of them so much as losing his foot apparel. *¡Increíble! Estás bullshitando,* amigo. You're bullshitting me, I said.

He gave that dopey grin again and shrugged his shoulders in a "what can be done about these things?" kind of way. Then his smile fell to pieces when the constable arrived to see what we were doing.

I apologized to Ciro. *Lo siento.* It was not my intention to have you arrested. I'm just doing my job and they saw what was happening. I'm sure you understand?

*No te preocupes,* he assured me. Don't be troubled. This is only my second time being caught. They will only send me back home over there. I will try ten more times until I make it. As I have before.

You might die, I told him.

I've got six children, friend.

I looked across the Rio Grande to the point on the shore where Ciro said they began their swim. There were factories there, in the background, their gleaming metallic roofs and smokestacks lighting up in the falling sun.

*¿Por qué no trabajas allí?* Why don't you just get a job over there on your side?

*¿Allí?* He laughed. There? You cannot get work there. Those are the American factories. The maquiladoras. You have to know somebody in there to get a job. It's all fixed. Besides, they don't pay much. They work you and then throw you away. He broke into his smile again: No, it's much better to try on this side, amigo.

American factories? Of course. Yes, thank you for the education, Ciro. And good luck.

NAFTA. I counted the years. Yes, NAFTA was celebrating its twentieth anniversary. And CAFTA, the Central American Free Trade Agreement, was about ten years old. We were promised better wages. We were promised the flow of illegal immigration would dry up. Free trade would raise all boats. That was the promise. The reality here in the heat was that a pregnant woman from a sinking-boat nation somewhere south of here was making a mad dash for the American border on a Sea-Doo and two guys in the back of a squad car had little more than a pair of flip-flops and a half dozen mouths to feed.

# Gray Donkeys/*Burros Grises*

REYNOSA, MEXICO—

We needed to get out of McAllen and into Mexico with our cameras. We needed to get a look at those American factories, talk to those workers, see how they lived. But neighboring Reynosa, just over the border, was awash in blood. With narco-wars raging between Mexican cartels, the U.S. government had shuttered its consulate there months ago. In fact, just a few days before we arrived in Texas, ten people had been slaughtered in a midday Reynosa shootout. Our TV company insisted that if we were considering a trip into Mexico, we would need security—which we didn't have, which we couldn't afford, and which the company was silent about providing. We didn't have legitimate press credentials, for fuck's sake.

When you cover a foreign conflict as a reporter, there are times you move with security. Most times you work with an interpreter and driver. Sometimes you just wing it. It's a gut decision. I have known and worked with journalists who have been killed in action, others maimed, still others kidnapped and held for ransom. But those are the chances you take for the story if you feel the story is important enough, something worthy of history. Of course, these journalists I speak of are generally writers and photographers. TV is a whole different deal, a different mind-set. A little less brave. A little more stagecrafted.

Besides, Reynosa wasn't a far-flung outpost of the waning American Empire somewhere on foreign sands where you couldn't speak the language and couldn't drink the water—okay, maybe it was a better idea not to drink the water, but you still could. This was essentially home. I had a responsibility to cut through the artifice of the TV reports, the repetition of unchallenged facts, the amplification of partisan bullshit. Seeing is believing.

We'd gotten pictures of hungry children in holding pens and the rotting remains of a migrant in the bush who would be buried in a pauper's grave without his name. Was I going to be afraid to walk into Mexico? For Chrissake, old women crossed back and forth at all hours of the night on the pedestrian bridge, pushing shopping carts stuffed with foot creams and snack cakes. Hardly.

But with the violence raging, I was going to need somebody who knew where to go. Or better still, who knew where *not* to go. After all, it'd be hard to explain to corporate how our rental van and cameras went missing down south. So I called a guy who knew a guy who might know a guy.

At high noon, there was a heavy knock on our motel room door. I cracked it a sliver. Stale, feverish air billowed in from the parking lot. A huge bearlike silhouette stood in the frame, back-lighted by the sun. I opened the door a little wider.

Poncho?

Yes.

He stepped into the room and offered his hand, which was as big as a lesser man's foot. He was well over six feet tall and easily three hundred pounds, with a goatee and shaved skull. What was odd was the leather coat. It must have been a hundred degrees outside and he was wearing a thin leather. His scalp was beaded with perspiration. I looked for something to give him. The pickings were slim.

The motel tap water came from the Rio Grande, which begins two thousand miles away in Durango, Colorado. By the time it arrived at the motel faucet in McAllen, it had absorbed farm pesticides, street runoff, factory chemicals, and dogshit along its path across the western Plains. And so the heavily treated tap water tasted like a rag soaked in formaldehyde. I had little else to give. We had drunk all the beer.

Whiskey? I offered.

Don't mind if I do.

Ice?

Certainly.

The room was full of our cigarette vapors that hung on the thin rays of sunlight bleeding through the window blinds, creating a milky, dreamlike atmosphere. The ice cubes tinkled. The air conditioner rattled.

This mountain of a man was Poncho Ortiz, the baddest motherfucker in these parts who didn't make a living killing or smuggling or arresting people. He was the only reporter I knew of covering the drug cartels in real time, and he was working both sides of the border to do it. Very dangerous indeed.

As far as the narco-war went, most American journalists were not reporting on it. Except for Poncho here, who was leaning against the wall, refusing a chair, sweating in his leather like he was in a Tarantino picture, but cooler because he was real.

How did he do it? How did he maneuver through a corpse-strewn gangland without having his testicles stuffed down his throat? It's not as though a man of this size could hide behind a tree. Reporters as a matter of routine die on the border. It was balls. Big balls. And desire. *Respeto, loco malparido.* Respect, crazy bastard.

So you want to go to Reynosa? He chuckled. I don't recommend it, to be honest.

He regaled us with stories of executions, decapitations, rape. The Gulf Cartel, he said, was at war with the Los Zetas cartel, and at war with itself. There was too much money involved. The cartels were responsible for the mass graves, the corpses in the bakery ovens, the hands and feet without bodies. It was so bad, Poncho said, that the largest American newspapers from Brownsville to McAllen to Laredo had forbidden their reporters to cross the border. Reporters die, remember. At least the Mexican ones. More than a hundred in the past decade alone, making Mexico the most perilous place to be a journalist in the world, after Afghanistan. Those who wanted to live, Poncho told us, were required to clear their stories with the cartel's director of media relations.

Media relations? Really? I looked at Bob, who looked at Matt, who looked at me.

Yes, really, Poncho assured us. It's no spring break, man.

I thought for a moment. Decapitations and directors of media relations notwithstanding, we needed to go. I was more afraid of losing my job for going to Mexico than my life. But it was an important story and disobeying unspoken directives from unseen executives is how you scraped the good stories together.

Okay, I said to Poncho, can you make a call?

Poncho made a call.

. . .

The next morning, Poncho pulled into the motel lot in his beater. Matt, with two young children and no travel documents, would stay in McAllen and collect B-roll for our story. Bob would come with me, bringing the smaller, more unassuming camera. He was excited. In the past, Bob had jumped out on a highway to impede the getaway of a crooked congressman. He had steered a car through a ghetto shootout with one hand while holding the camera in his second and taking a drag off a cigarette with his third. Bob, in short, liked trouble.

You brought the small cameras? Good, Poncho said. Once we're in Mexico, we're going to meet a man. He will pull up in a van. You will move quickly. You will say and do nothing until you are in the van. Understood?

No problem, Bob replied.

We cleared customs with Poncho telling the agent we were going for a beer. He then parked in a public garage in Reynosa and we walked to the town square, sat on a bench, and waited. Bob, wearing his do-rag and safari shorts, pulled out a camera and began shooting random signage.

Poncho elbowed me in the ribs. What the fuck?

Bob, I whispered. What the fuck?

What the fuck? Bob shrugged. He put the camera down and lit a smoke. A white van crept up from the corner. The back doors popped open.

*Vamonos. Buena suerte.* Good luck.

And like that, we were careening through the moribund streets of Reynosa. The boulevards were wide, the architecture bleak. Military pickups barreled through traffic with masked federal agents

in the beds manning mounted machine guns, part of the army's occupation of a city of anarchy. A drone hovered over the horizon
looking for God knows who or what. We followed it for a while, until
it banked and turned out of sight.

The driver was a man named Leo, a former journalist who calculated it was better for his breathing to retire before he was forced
to stop breathing. He took us to a corner where ten had died in a gun
battle a week earlier. There was no mention of it in the American
papers. There were still bloodstains on the sidewalk. Bob ventured
a few frames. No problem. People went about their business.

Next, we went to a mission enclosed by stucco walls and a sliding
iron gate. It housed a Christian ministry that tended to Central
American women and children, stranded and penniless. The
Rio Grande meandered just behind its northern wall. And behind
that, the international bridge to the promised land was in plain,
mocking view.

Ingrid Bran and her two toddlers were staying here. When she
heard that Obama was granting amnesty, she had scraped together
$150, left Honduras, and crossed into Mexico from Guatemala by
raft. She and her boys took a series of uneventful bus rides to
Reynosa, where they finally ran out of money. She has family in Mi-
ami, she said, but doesn't have money for a smuggler to raft them
into the United States. I gave her $20 for food, wondering if she
would use it to buy an inner tube and cross the narrow stretch of
river just outside the wall, throw her hands up, and ask for three
one-way tickets to Little Havana.

We then drove through the slums where workers from the maquiladoras, the big American-owned factories, lived in cinder-block
shacks. The roofs were corrugated metal. There was no plumbing or
running water. Electricity came from a shared power cord; the

toilet was a plastic bucket. The sanitation man arrived via donkey-drawn cart. The streets were made of dust.

As we filmed out the van window, Leo asked a woman what work she did. She assembled air-conditioning motors, she replied. She was pretty in a worn, sunken way, with large, sad, troubled eyes—a darker, living version of Dorothea Lange's migrant mother. An older boy sat in the back of the shack.

Leo asked to see her pay stub. It was very First World—neatly printed, with purple letterhead, much like a W-9 form in the United States. Leo calculated the exchange rate on his smartphone. The woman earned $1.15 an hour. The official word from the American companies and the Mexican government was that the average wage for a Mexican worker in an "American" plant was $5–$6 an hour. That was plainly bullshit.

Then consider that the official Mexican minimum wage was 58 cents an hour. By that standard, this woman was clearly earning more than many Mexicans, twice as much in fact.

At the same time, however, the U.S. federal minimum wage was $7.25 an hour—or twelve and a half times greater than Mexico's (Guatemala's, by comparison, was $1.20 an hour, Honduras's $1). Now imagine if American workers were able to export themselves to another country and earn the equivalent of $90 an hour, or $190,000 a year, inseminating sheep by hand. Forget the North Dakota oil patch. Hello, Calgary!

Somewhere in this disparity of compensation lies the seemingly unsolvable riddle of human migration. Six dollars an hour? Who was really verifying the "facts" provided by these miserly swine living it up in their pop-up palaces behind the iron gates? It's no wonder the trade pact didn't stop the flow of immigrants. It was the mathematics of the thing. She could earn twelve times as much tending the gardens of a U.S. congressman while her father's farm collapsed, unable to compete with American subsidized corn.

NAFTA no good, Leo said to us in a Spanglish patois. The people live . . . *como un burro*. Like a donkey.

We bounced along the rutted road in the panel van, then turned onto smooth pavement four lanes wide, which led us through Factory Row. Neat, new facilities with green lawns and plenty of security guards and surveillance cameras. There was Caterpillar from Illinois. Corning from New York. Textile plants from the South. And wait. What is that? Delphi. The auto-parts maker from Flint, Michigan, that used to be a division of General Motors.

Flint. My corner of the planet, where people now lived like burros.

Fuck, croaked Bob from the back of the van, which was now as hot as a barbecue pit. That's my dad's old company.

The enormity of it hit home. Cartels and hungry children. Gun battles and filthy water. Border patrols and masked *federales*. A buck-fifteen an hour and a pail to shit in. We fell silent under the weight of it all. Bob wiped his eyes. I'm not sure if it was perspiration that was making them red.

Leo dropped us at the border, we had that beer, then walked back into the United States. Matt was idling there near the hurricane fencing lining the border.

How'd it go?

We gotta get home to Flint, man, I said. I'm starting to get the picture.

# Red Teeth

There must have been a run on Kool-Aid, because everybody in the trailer park seemed to be drinking it. The old man in Unit 1420, the kids playing in the rubble pile of an old double-wide that had been torn down and left to rot, the little white baby hanging out a window with a load in his diaper. Everyone residing at the Kirkwood mobile home park wearing teeth stained red. Except Dee Johnson, a fifty-year-old white woman. It didn't appear as though Dee was wearing her teeth today.

What's with the Kool-Aid? I asked.

The tap water looked and tasted like crap, she told me. The city had switched the water from its Detroit source for some reason. Now the city was drawing its drinking water from the toxic Flint River. Officials assured the people it was okay, but still you couldn't drink the water without sugar in it. It made you gag.

There was a brownfield out behind the trailer with the toddler hanging from the window there on Sunshine Drive, a square mile of cement and horse thistle and weedy trees. One square mile of post-industrial nothingness. This is where Delphi used to make things in America: spark plugs, fuel pumps, oil gauges, speedometers. It also pumped out paychecks: more than ten thousand paychecks a week at the plant's peak. Plus bennies. Good bennies. And bennies were where it was at.

Delphi was a division of General Motors before GM spun it off in the late 1990s to save money. That's when Delphi became a stand-alone company. But the financial sleight of hand couldn't save it, and Delphi, the largest auto-parts manufacturer in the world, declared bankruptcy in 2005, sending shock waves through the automobile industry.

Delphi ditched its pension obligations onto the American tax-payer as workers' pay was cut in half and executives took millions in bonuses. The company then received billions in federal bailout dollars, shuttered most of its American factories, and moved its corporate headquarters to England to avoid paying taxes to the U.S. Treasury.

At the moment Delphi declared bankruptcy, it had employed fifty thousand American workers. Less than a decade later, it employed more than fifty thousand Mexican workers, making it one of the biggest employers in Mexico, with factories in hellholes like Reynosa. And it left behind abandoned city blocks in places like Flint.

Predictably, Flint—Vehicle City—hit the skids. Murder City. Police headquarters closed on the weekends. Failing schools. Four in ten living in poverty. It all got turned on its head somehow. Flint: Can't drink the water. Delphi: *Hecho en México*.

Flint is the birthplace of General Motors and the United Auto Workers and mass credit. For years the factories hummed, and the

Flint River grew so toxic with industrial waste, it was said you could clean brass with it. But Flint was rich. It didn't need the river. It could afford to ship one in from Detroit, sixty miles away. But then Flint's jobs went to Mexico and Flint's politicians mismanaged and stole. And Vehicle City went broke. People left by the tens of thousands.

The city was taken over by the state in 2011 and stripped of its assets to pay off its debt. In order to save more money, the governor's men ordered the people who were left to drink from the Flint River.

The children's lips would have told you it couldn't be drunk without Kool-Aid.

Down the road from the collapsing trailer-court cracker box was another brownfield, another dead factory, where dead-end children with blood-red teeth rummaged through filth. None of them had a chance.

Would somebody get that kid out of the window? I thought. He's gonna fall and break his neck! And for fuck's sake, change his fucking diaper, won't you please?

Unemployment and homicide—that's about what they got left in Flint, said Dee, who grew up here and raised kids here and grew irrelevant here. Irrelevant to the government. Irrelevant to the powers that be. Irrelevant but still alive.

The old footprint of a factory long gone. The jobs somewhere else, done by someone else being paid peanuts, or done by a machine that requires no peanuts, no health insurance, no time card. It hurt to look at. I grew up near a Ford transmission plant. Bob worked at GM for a few years, and his father clocked thirty with the company. By the end, his old man was the guy helping the factories relocate to Mexico, set them up, and get them running. He regrets it now. But damn it, somebody was going to do it.

These plants literally put food in our bellies and muscle on our bones and good schools in our communities. They were part of our fiber. Sure, guys like me and Bob and Matt, who grew up near the steel foundries of Gary, Indiana, moved up and on and out. We became men of the world, but we are the offspring of heavy-metal industry.

And so was Dee. Dee here was our sister. Her children, our children. She looked too old for herself. She'd been made into a Third World woman while the *campesina* back in Reynosa had been transformed into a prisoner of a sweltering box deep in a slum of the new world economy.

Evoking concepts of comparative advantage and opportunity costs, the ruling bosses promised that the new way of doing things would be good for people like Dee and the children running wild here: free trade and a new public water source. But surely it wasn't. You could watch the water come from the tap. It didn't just look like shit, it probably had actual shit in it.

Still, they were telling the people the water was fine to wash your babies in. The economy was improving, they said. And those Central American women and children on TV bum-rushing the border? Well, they said, we had room for that desperate horde because we were a generous people.

But what about *us*? asked people like Dee. What about *our* kids? We do everything for those kids from over there, but what about *our* kids here?

No one's listening, sister.

Delphi had announced the previous week that it had earned record profits. But where were these profits? Not in this bombed-out trailer court. Not in the U.S. Treasury accounts. I tried repeatedly to get an appointment with Rod O'Neal, the CEO of Delphi, but couldn't get ahold of him. Or rather, he refused to see us. But this is TV, and paper statements of corporate doublespeak tend to be bad for ratings. Did Delphi owe anything to the American people? Was it an American company anymore? Would it pay back the bailout and pension obligations now that the money was rolling in? How was Rod O'Neal going to spend that $14.8 million in salary and bonuses? How about a twenty-four-pack of Huggies for the kid in 1511? It seemed like the least he could do.

We took a drive to Delphi's "operational headquarters," about a half hour down Interstate 75, in suburban Detroit, where Rod has his offices. Hot Rod, I decided, was going to have to tell it to the lens.

Never come empty-handed, my mother always taught me. Bring a gift of some sort, a token of esteem and affection. So we stopped at a chain convenience store. Browsing through the merchandise: shoelaces from Bangladesh, condoms made in India, even the goddamned store's corporate headquarters were located in Asia. Eventually, I found just the right gift: a microwaveable chimichanga "assembled in Mexico."

How appropriate, Bob said, cackling. I bet O'Neal's gonna love it.

Delphi's so-called global administrative office is a big ugly pillbox of a building laid down in a sprawling blacktop parking lot off the cloverleaf ribbon of interstate, located near absolutely nothing. This is where the white establishment works. The suits. The outsourcers. The brains of the global conglomerate. Except Mr. O'Neal, of course. He's black. So Delphi deserved diversity points, I figured.

We got lost in the sprawl, until we got found. It was an eerie campus. There was no sign of life. No movement. No people. No birds on the well-tended lawns.

We entered the main building. Again security. Again hubbub about the cameras. Again the recurrent question. Credentials?

Yes, indeed. Sure. NEWS MEDIA PRESS OFFICIAL IDENTIFICATION.

A corporate mouthpiece wearing an ill-fitting sleeveless blouse and surrounded by security booted us out, but not before accepting the chimichanga on Rod's behalf.

I should have also brought him some bottled water, because soon after we visited, this notice was published:

---

### CITY OF FLINT

**LOCALIZED DRINKING WATER WARNING**

*A localized area of City of Flint water is contaminated with fecal coliform*

**BOIL YOUR WATER BEFORE USING**

---

# White Is the New Black

In Flint, at least the children had access to water. In Detroit, they were being forced to steal it. The Motor City was under state emergency management and trying to dig its way out of the largest municipal bankruptcy in American history. The search for revenue left no stone unturned, no crevice unsearched, no couch cushion unmolested. The slashing of pensions and health benefits for public employees. Cutbacks of overtime and holiday pay for cops. Firefighters doing double duty as EMTs. The selling off of toll tunnels and municipal parking lots.

The sheriff had also cometh, putting thousands of families on the streets for failing to pay their property taxes (or, more often, the slumlord failing to pay). People packed themselves into houses like rodents, neighbors and relatives and sometimes perfect strangers sharing apartments, rooms, closets, or even driveways, where old women slept unprotected in their vans. It was either that or squat. Thousands of people had broken into unoccupied homes and claimed them. Jump the power box for electricity, bypass the gas meter with a hacksaw and rubber tubing, and you're cooking. At least until the cops show or the house blows.

But then the city took away the life source itself. It shut off water service to fifteen thousand households due to lack of payment, with tens of thousands more scheduled in the coming months. No one was spared who was sixty days in arrears—not the elderly, not the invalids, not the babies.

In an East Side neighborhood, a young black woman named Letishia was bathing her child in a plastic tub in her front yard, the water pilfered from an abandoned home next door that had tall grass and no windows but, ironically, still had water service. It was a sweltering afternoon, and I rinsed my head in the hose that was on perpetual flow. Word travels quickly, and people from the block who'd had their water cut came and went. Milk jugs. Gardening pails. Spackling buckets. Like a tribe of Bedouins to a well, except this tribe was too poor to afford camels to carry them away.

Downtown Detroit was a different story. Downtown was booming with investment made by billionaires who were given generous tax breaks and public subsidies. Downtown, white people were moving back. The lofts were at capacity. A white man had been elected mayor for the first time in forty years because he carried a sheen of competency. The Horace Dodge Fountain was full of coins. There were new restaurants and bars and art galleries, tennis-shoe shops and fashion boutiques, and too many T-shirts with slogans: "Detroit v Everybody," "Detroit Hustles Harder," "Imported from Detroit," "Comeback City," and so on.

Sandboxes and basketball courts and food trucks had sprung up to amuse the millennials who worked for Dan Gilbert, the Quicken

Loans mortgage mogul who was buying up dozens of ghost buildings in the city's core and moving his people and businesses into them. At the same time, his company was being sued by the Department of Justice for tens of millions of dollars, accused of pumping up borrowers' income or credit scores and pushing appraisers to fudge the appraisals of homes in order to make underqualified applicants eligible for federal housing insurance.

Property tax revenue was being diverted from the bankrupt, crumbling Detroit public school system to subsidize a new professional hockey arena for the billionaire Ilitch family, who owned the Detroit Red Wings, the Detroit Tigers, the Little Caesars pizza chain, and the Motor City casino.

The Red Wings were late on their water bill too, but the city did nothing to them. Hey, you can't have ice without water.

I watched from behind the rim of a three-dollar cup of premium coffee as adult hipsters at some sort of Quicken bonding seminar shrieked with delight as they ran among the sandboxes, pelting each other with water balloons. It was all a great laugh. It was the comeback story.

It was more precisely a tale of two cities. The small well-to-do white core sweeping in on the great broom of gentrification, blithely unaware of the great, heaving, Dickensian black outskirts swelling and breathless with discontent. It was like a ravenous man staring through the window, fogging the plate glass as another dug into his lamb ragù with root vegetables, farm fresh to table (actually a quite delicious and popular dish in one of the new high-end restaurants not a block from the skid row warming center). Scenes like this were common in the new Detroit.

What about us? Letishia asked back in the black, ramshackle neighborhood, echoing what Dee had said to me in the white ramshackle trailer park. We don't got something as simple as water. You don't got no water, you die. Is that what they want? My baby to die? Because we're poor?

I had no answer except to say the poor could not afford to pay and the rich refused to pay. So imagine the hostilities from those in the middle, increasingly squeezed to take up the slack from the poles. Imagine when the great middle has had enough.

In the meantime, the ghetto was going to explode. I could feel it. The ghetto was going to blow first and the trailer park second. The ghetto always feels it first. Poverty, joblessness, disinvestment, incarceration. Abandoned and walled off, poor black people always catch hell first. That's the totem of American life. Without water or hope in a sultry summer season, emotions in the poorest big city in America were on high boil. Something was going to give. And I would be proven right in just a few days. It's just that I picked the wrong city. It wouldn't be Detroit, but Ferguson, Missouri.

*The real reason that nonviolence is considered to be a virtue in Negroes . . . is that white men do not want their lives, their self-image, or their property threatened.*

—JAMES BALDWIN

In an attempt to explain the African experience in Missouri, a black man named Charles told me a thread of the following story. We were standing in a suburb of St. Louis, at the site of a looting and arson in response to the police killing of an unarmed black teenager.

The first known record of the phrase "sold down the river" comes from the journal of a Missouri cabinet maker from 1835. In it, a slave named Elies learns he is to be sold to a plantation farther down the Mississippi River, where life in the cotton fields was especially brutal. Elies becomes so frenzied at this news that he first attempts to sever his legs, then slit his own throat before successfully drowning himself in a river.

It sounded like an old-timey hand-me-down tale, but I made a note of it. Sold Me Down the River. When I returned home to the North, I looked it up. It was true, reminding me that the American is generally poorly instructed of his own history, not because it is especially difficult to learn, but rather, because it is difficult to hear.

Charles claimed that Missouri was the last state to abolish slavery. I admit, I had to look that one up too. They teach so little history in America. His Missouri slavery claim was also true—to a point.

*When Abraham Lincoln signed the Emancipation Proclamation in 1863 he granted freedom to slaves of the Confederate states. There were, however, five border states nominally loyal to the Union that also permitted slavery. In order to keep Delaware, Maryland, Kentucky, West Virginia, and Missouri aligned with the North, Lincoln did not release from bondage the slaves in those states for two more years.*

*That's the history. Charles then offered his vision of the future of greater St. Louis, Missouri, with a sweep of his hand across the embers and glass, his young son cradled in his arm.*

*Once the media is gone, he said, St. Louis County [police] ain't gonna forget this.*

*Once the coast was clear and things got back to normal, Charles felt, the cops around here were going to beat some black ass just to even things out.*

*And for that, and for the sake of his boy, Charles was already laying his plans for a move up the river.*

# St. Louis Blues

We went airborne like Steve McQueen in *Bullitt*. Except this wasn't a '68 Fastback, it was a tired old SUV that made funny noises and had too many miles on it. I was hauling ass uphill but didn't know there was a steep drop-off in the road, which cut through the north end of town. We hit the hill's peak at eighty miles an hour, maybe, and were launched airborne at an angle. We would either take out the light pole or plow through the vestibule of the church beyond it. The vestibule may have been the preferred outcome. First responders are usually busy during a riot. Plow through a church, and the carnage could prove so spectacular that an ambulance just might arrive in time to save your lives. But two reporters wrapped around a light pole? Take two aspirin and call me in the morning, son.

Ohhh fuuuck!! Matt and I squalled like duct-taped tomcats as we touched down, clipped the curb, bounced twice, and righted the truck, avoiding misadventure altogether. Getting off the accelerator, we crept up to the corner of Ferguson's West Florissant Avenue, where we could see fresh flames erupt and masked figures dancing in the shadows.

We had been to this corner earlier in the day, when thousands came out to celebrate the police pullout after a long, ugly week of military-style occupation. The twisted remnants of the burned-out QuickTrip gas station were dark, banners still hanging on the chain-link fence now surrounding it: "Hands Up! Don't Shoot!"

The gas station had been a victim of innuendo and whisper, a rumor ricocheting through the apartment complex nearby that someone who worked there had called the police and said eighteen-year-old Michael Brown, a black man, had robbed the place.

Whether the rumor was true or not, the cops had arrived, setting in motion a series of disputed events that ended with the unarmed Brown lying dead in the street, plugged six times—in the head, chest, arm, and hand—by a white officer's gun.

*Burn the motherfucker to the ground!* the chant went up. A bacchanalia of fire erupted. The looting of rims and tires by a couple assholes whetted the press's appetite, and cable news started playing up that angle. *The animals.*

Then came the martial response, the tear gas and jackboots, the masked police officers dressed like SEAL Team Six. The curfews and the riot shields. The no-loitering rule and the arrests. It was a shitshow tailor-made for the ravenous and bottomless news maw.

In the days that followed, the QuickTrip had become a shrine, a sanctum, the Nicanor Gate of a movement. Ministers, gangsters, elderly curiosity seekers, politicians, and neighborhood children came to gather, pray, discuss, gossip, to exchange conspiracies, bits of news, and mutual affirmations, and to conduct interviews with the media.

Media, so much media. A spectacle! A big-top news circus broadcasting live from the scene 24/7, with reporters in the requisite makeup* and khaki, impromptu sets erected in the parking lots of storage garages and Chinese restaurants. No story too small. Come one, come all. A mime troupe came by to stage a silent play for the cameras' benefit, and then a break-dancing company. And why not? This is a terrible tragedy, but one can't turn down free publicity. Ferguson is part of America, don't you know?

And yet serious things were discussed here. The outrage at Ferguson and St. Louis police. "Black while driving"—it was absolutely understood that four black men to a car is dangerous for your health if you're one of the black men in the car. The backwardness of Missouri, the cracker land of all cracker lands, one of the last states to give up the institution of slavery, which, in the minds and daily experiences of those convened here, never fully went away. The man always had his boot on your head. The lockups and beatdowns, the court fines. A modern-day peonage. The county jail just a different version of the old convict lease system.

I'm proud of my people, a young, excitable man named Brian told me of the burning and pillaging. It was an anthem, he said. A black fist. A cry for attention. Payback for Trayvon Martin. (The unarmed seventeen-year-old black kid had been killed not by a cop but by a half-white, half-Latino dope working the neighborhood watch shift. Still, close enough.)

Then there was Eric Garner getting choked out by police just for trying to sell loose cigarettes for a buck in Staten Island, New York, a town where cigarettes go for fourteen dollars a pack. He was trying to feed six kids. Why not write him a ticket for loitering? Why you got to choke him out? An economic situation turned into a racial standoff turned into another corpse of a black man.

And then there's Rodney. You can never forget Rodney King.

---

* It is not very well known that the foundation of men's TV makeup is women's makeup. I refuse to wear it.

Y'all saw it. The beatdown. Now, Brian explained, St. Louis gots Michael. This one's ours, this shit goes back to slavery, and we're gonna get our justice.

The eruption was a spontaneous, violent appeal for a stake in this thing called America. And if men like Brian and Charles and Kerwin and Delmont who were hanging out at the QuickTrip didn't get it, then the whole of metropolitan St. Louis—white and black and Arab—would burn. That was a promise. As for the tires and rims that were looted last time around? Fuck it, Brian said. That's beside the point. Just a little booty to go along with the justice, a tithing for the high priests of disobedience.

I wish I woulda been here . . . You wanna hit this here blunt?

There was an awakening here in outer St. Louis, and a dead eighteen-year-old who had his hands up was the deliverance. Whether Michael Brown really did have his hands up was still a matter of contention. It was clear he had no weapon. But if his friend was going to stand there in the hot summer sun and tell everybody on cable TV that he did have his hands up and cable TV was going to broadcast it unchecked? Then that's the way it happened, at least to the black community here. Michael had his hands up. He was executed. That's what Brian and his friends believed, anyway.

There were, of course, two versions: the black version and the white version. The cop shot the kid in the back, unprovoked, while he had his hands up; he'd been stopped in the middle of the street for no reason other than that he was black. That was one.

The second version—the white version—went that the imposing three-hundred-pound man, who had strong-armed the QuickTrip convenience store minutes earlier, attacked the cop. This version went that the officer had simply asked the young man and his friend to remove themselves from the middle of the street and kindly use the sidewalk. Brown freaked, punched the cop, and reached for the officer's gun. Fearing for his life, the officer, naturally, had to use deadly force.

Either way, shamefully, Brown's body lay for more than four hours in the street in front of the Canfield Green apartments under the August sun, the police not even bothering to cover him with a sheet. People looked on, whispered among themselves, whispered some more, and it began to brew.

Cops beating ass and dropping unarmed black men, that was nothing new here in Missouri, or anywhere in America. But something else was also afoot in Ferguson, another instigator, something unseen yet tangible and hard-fisted. A larger, more menacing enemy.

The Government.

Ferguson couldn't afford itself. The bureaucracy was too big for the tax base. The city hall and the police department remained overwhelmingly white while the town, over the last decade, had changed color.

In order to balance its books, the city leaders did not slash their own jobs or significantly pare their budgets. Instead, they decided to shake down Ferguson's residents. And they used the police to do it. Two-thirds of Ferguson was black, but 90 percent of the police force was white and 85 percent of police stops were of blacks; 90 percent of searches were of blacks and 95 percent of arrests were of blacks, even though studies by the state and federal governments showed that whites were more likely to be carrying contraband while driving.

In addition, a full 95 percent of citations for driving while distracted, failure to comply, or a strange offense until then unknown to me—"manner of walking"—were issued to blacks.

According to a Department of Justice report, when Ferguson's courts collected more than $2 million in 2012, doubling the haul from the previous year, the city manager, who was white, fired off an email to the police chief, who was also white: "Awesome! Thanks!"

But you didn't have to tell this to young black men like Brian. They lived it. The exorbitant court fees, the penalties for late payment, getting your ass beat by deputies in lockup and then being charged for the cost of cleaning your blood off the deputies' uniforms were too much for any man to stand. Add in a dead teenager lying for four hours on a skillet-hot street and you've got yourself the makings of a civil disturbance.

The government isn't for the people, Brian said, now sipping on a gin and juice. I don't know where he got it. He just got it. Not just the cocktail, but the philosophy.

The government is the *enemy* of the people. The government is eating the people alive. Sip?

Shit, I thought. He sounded like Carrie Dann on the high-desert plateau. Or Lil Dog out on the Bundy ranch. Or the old girl in the Flint trailer park. *The government is against me. Tyranny! Rage against the machine!*

Caving to the nightly pressure of TV cameras showing military policing methods in Ferguson, the authorities not only released the name of the officer who had shot Michael Brown—Darren Wilson—they also backed off and backed away, and the weeklong state of emergency was lifted, emboldening black people with the feeling that they had driven out the occupying force, a street gang in blue, the army of the *enemy*.

Gone were the armored personnel vehicles, the cops in camouflage and body armor staring through their scopes that can target out to five hundred meters, pointing 5.56mm rifles at citizens for no worthwhile reason. The governor even put a black man in charge of the police, Captain Roland Johnson of the state highway patrol. Under the captain's direction, officers allowed folks to stand on the sidewalk now as they pleased. And the people did. Gin and juice. Souped-up cars laying rubber in the road. Prayer circles. People wanting to show their children the *moment* it all happened. The victory. Cars backed up to the highway. The New Black Panthers directing traffic. A celebrity even showed up—but not as popular a figure around here as one might have thought.

*Fuck Jesse. Why he coming now? Where the fuck he been? Shit, posing for the cameras.*

*Fuck it, I'm gonna get me a picture. Hey Jesse! Lemme get a selfie!*

It was both peaceful and electric. For one brief, shining afternoon, it was a victory for the black side of St. Louis, a place short on wins.

And then darkness came.

We hung out on the corner until about eleven o'clock. All was peaceful, so we had gone back to the hotel to have something to eat and wash our faces. Then Matt called me in my room. He was watching looters on the local TV station. It was being broadcast by a camera far away with a powerful zoom lens. Not a cameraman worth his salt was willing to walk into the mayhem of Molotov cocktails and masked marauders swiping meat and hair extensions, liquor and premium-brand cigarettes.

We banged on Bob's door. He was out cold, sleeping, and could not be woken above his snoring. We left him in bed and barreled for West Florissant Avenue.

We pulled up just past the gas station, at the strip mall, aptly named, as it was being stripped clean. A new government had arisen in the void. A new grouping of imposed values. The mob. Locusts. Anarchy. Selfish destruction with no binding morality.

And who comes walking by just then, humming and happy, like he'd just gotten kissed at the homecoming dance? Brian! Good old Brian, out for a night of sightseeing. The cops got in their cars and left, he told us. Just got up and got gone. Motherfuckers.

He was right. The police were nowhere to be found. It must be some sort of mistake. The place was burning. So I called 911. Local dispatch referred me to the county police, but did not connect me. I called the county police, who referred me to the state police. I called the state police, who referred me back to the local police. It was a big "fuck you" to Ferguson. You want to fuck with us? they seemed to be saying. You want to burn your own shit down? Have at it.

Matt grabbed his giant P2 camera and tripod out of the SUV and began filming. The camera is much too big for a riot and has an eyepiece that requires one to place his temple against the casing, which creates a blind spot for the cameraman since he has one eye closed while he films, the other stuffed in the viewfinder, robbing him of his vision. The mob that Matt could not see ebbed and flowed around him, some attracted by the flames, some by the camera. Matt was occupied by the explosion of an incendiary bomb, which had shattered the plate glass of Sam's Meat Market & More. Flames started licking out of the window.

As Matt filmed, someone grabbed his camera by the lens.

Fuck off, Matt shouted.

It was a weasel of a little white guy. Masked. Dressed in black like a ninja. Except this was no Bruce Lee. He was a wisp, a ferret with a weak chin, a high-pitched nasal voice. He most likely belonged to one of those anarchist or anti-fascist left-wing groups that now seemed to jet into civil disturbances and break shit. A privileged white guy out for thrills, railing against a machine I suspected he was so much a part of.

Hey, man, stop filming, he squealed. That's snitchin'. You're snitchin', man! That's so uncool to be filming, man.

I shoved him in the chest. Don't touch the fucking camera, I said. And what the fuck are you doing here? You're a bucket of fucking chum. You're somebody's lunch if you don't be careful.

The crowd around us seemed to enjoy the spectacle, and the white kid moved on, muttering: That's snitchin', man . . . that's snitchin', man. I wondered if Daddy gave him an allowance.

Sitting on the steps of Sam's was another masked man, a large pistol stuffed in his waistband. This guy was the stereotypical Fear of a Black Planet come to life. He was long and muscular, dark as obsidian, handsome with dreadlocks. And the gun—that was the topper. He was shouting at a mob of about a dozen who were trying to make their way into the store. I signaled to Matt and we walked right into the beehive and sat down next to him.

You wouldn't know it using a long lens, but here on the steps, in the wan yellow light, a remarkable scene was playing out. The long dark man was no criminal, no looter. He was the only thing around that could pass as law and order. He was trying to keep the mob out of the Arabs' store.

Y'all ain't even from around here, he shouted at the looters. This shit's ignorant.

His name was DJ. He said he was from around here. He was raising a son around here. He shopped in this store. He didn't want some drunk assholes burning down his neighborhood. Or the world contorting his meaning of Ferguson, having images of looters supplanting the peaceful calls for justice earlier in the day.

Considering the seemingly selfish and cowardly behavior of the police, DJ was the only thing out here that represented order.

Some faces in the mob were masked with T-shirts, but their eyes glistened with booze and purpose. They looked at me and then said to DJ: You friends with the devil?

I'm friends with everybody, DJ answered with feeling. But we ain't gotta loot.

They inched toward the store, skulking like scavengers, daring DJ to plug one of them.

We gonna eat out of this motherfucker!

What could DJ do? Shoot them? What would that accomplish? More death. More ignominy to his community. He threw his hands in the air, muttered a few bitter words, and disappeared into the night.

With the pistol gone, the crowd emptied the store, then turned on us.

Turn the camera off, motherfucker!

I told Matt to keep filming. We weren't going to get run off that corner. We were going to do our job and then we were going to leave like men. It was our country too. My countrymen are not my enemies. Besides, we were on TV. Images matter. I wasn't going out looking like a pussy.

Looted bottles started flying, then batteries. A guy from nowhere emerged with a heavy orange traffic cone and hit me over the head. I stood my ground. Fighting or fleeing, either one could lead to a head stomping. You never know in a crowd. The dude took a swing at the camera and Matt, his face buried in the viewfinder, never saw it coming. The eyepiece snapped and the rioter slipped back into the mob. That's when a man, a black man, in leather gloves and a shirt as tight as a prophylactic, appeared from the recesses and ushered us back to our truck.

That's enough. You gotta go.

Thank you my brother.

Was the attack racially motivated? Did the crowd come at us because of our skin color, our hair texture, the way we carried ourselves? Did outsiders need to be pelted, cut, and beaten? Was this a payback for Michael Brown? Maybe, a little, I suppose. Again, this is America, remember. And color matters. But mostly, I figure the attack was based on the fact—and this is a provable fact—that people don't like being filmed while committing felonies.

The company was pleased. *Great footage!* They wanted us to make a black-mob-attacks-white-reporters internet clip. But Matt and I and bleary-eyed Bob all agreed we would not racebait. The story was DJ, not the beatdown. We wanted to provide a positive image, if such a thing could be said to exist amid the looting and rioting. There was something deeper there, something with a conscience, something with a higher truth. Things might be fucked up in America, but we could fix them. America is the greatest experiment in the history of humankind, a nation composed of tribes striving to overcome ancient impulses, a society improving itself through reason rather than destroying itself through violence.

I choose to believe we are more like DJ than the few dozen dumbasses stealing and burning. The poetry of the man, his manner and grace of speech, his bravery in a dark place, where the world would never suspect it. That was the story. He was the majority in Ferguson. It may have cost us a few million YouTube clicks, but it was the truth.

Bob was crestfallen the following day. He was taking it hard that he'd snored through the evening's mayhem.

Don't worry, man, apnea's a bitch, I said. You really should see a doctor about it, though.

Aw, shit, he moaned. I really feel bad.

Don't worry, man, I repeated, pointing to the TV behind the hotel bar. Look.

Missouri governor Jay Nixon was at a local church announcing that the state of emergency would be back in effect that evening at midnight: "This is a test. The eyes of the world are watching."

This guy's a real marshmallow, Bob said.

Yeah, he's on again, off again, I said. Send in the commandos. Pull them out. Let the town burn. You don't think St. Louis and Ferguson know that? You don't think they're coming out tonight?

It was a sure bet they were coming out tonight. Over at the concierge desk, the retinue of the Right Reverend Al Sharpton was already checking in. It was on. The riot and the shitshow. Welcome in, Al.

That evening, there was a heavy police presence in Ferguson, and West Florissant was completely blocked off to traffic. We pulled up to a county officer at a gas station that marked the perimeter and produced the credential: NEWS MEDIA PRESS OFFICIAL IDENTIFICATION.

He looked at us with an eyebrow raised.

You wanna go in there? he asked, incredulous.

It's the job.

Suit yourself. But I'm warning you, there's no telling if they're going to behave like animals. You're on your own.

The crowd was pulsing, expectant, hostile, black. The media was there, a swarm of them, white. We stood under the awning of a boarded-up chop suey joint, readying our gear, game planning, convincing ourselves to stay out of the way—no meddling, no heroics. A man out at this hour is a menace. Who else would be out at this hour? Good people are home in bed, their doors locked, their televisions tuned to this.

A group of strong-looking young men were muttering among themselves: *Some motherfucker's getting hurt tonight.* Malik Shabazz, the national chairman of the New Black Panther Party, seemed to take them at their word and implored the men through a bullhorn to please respect the curfew: No violence, my brothers! Please go home!

Ultimately, it wasn't Shabazz who convinced them, but seemingly God himself. Minutes before the curfew deadline was to take effect, the heavens opened and heavy rains began to fall. Almost instantly, West Florissant Avenue was washed clean and largely deserted. But not completely. A few dozen of the most devout remained. And wait . . . Who is that bebopping along the avenue, sippy cup in hand, humming and shouting, palm slapping and sightseeing, taking in the evening scenery?

It was good old Brian! He gave a wide smile. Take it easy, baby, he said. Take it slow. Get home safe. And off he disappeared into the crowd.

The police had once again mustered in armored vehicles at the south end of the avenue, the protesters massed to the north. Bob went west near the beauty shop and Matt and I to the east behind the rampart of the Chinese restaurant. At precisely midnight the rain stopped as quickly as it had come and the imperious voice of power, a white voice, booming through some unseen loudspeaker: *You must disperse immediately. Now! This is an order. You are subject to arrest or other actions.*

The most rowdy, committed, and possessed mocked the police. *Here's the finger, motherfucker! Here's a rock, cocksucker! No justice, no peace, bitches!*

They were egged on, encouraged, enticed by the gaggle of media, white reporters with cameras and recording devices who were making stars of them, instantly live-streaming their antics across the planet. And the protesters knew it; they began shouting not at the police but into the lenses. Just lay some music under it and you'd have had yourself a rap video.

Five hundred yards away, flanked to the east of the police, were the less adventurous members of the media, mostly mainstream, who weren't about to risk their good clothes in the muck and lather of the street. They stood behind metal barricades in the parking lot at McDonald's, looking from a distance like veal calves in a holding pen. This was the official "media section," where one could observe the action under the protection of the local police force. And Christ, what seats for the shitshow!

The reporters in the street filming the protesters had their backs to the police, conspicuously exposed and vulnerable but knowing full well that the cops would not open up on them. When all is said and done, white people, even the liberal ones, trust authority, have a deep-seated belief in it. The police would not blast a group of them. They knew it. Somewhere in there lies privilege.

The black protesters understood the racial calculus as well. With the mob of white reporters as a protective buffer, they grew bolder. Those hiding in the shadows drifted back onto the street. Soon they were throwing objects, taunting the police to let it rip. No one was backing down.

Clearly, TV was making things worse. Being a reporter requires some common sense and responsibility, but all that seemed to have vanished into the night.

Shut it down, a reporter from Texas shouted to his cameraman. He turned to me: This is disgusting.

It was. I liked the man and shook his hand. We too had stopped filming the protesters for that very reason. But we had not stopped filming the scene. We backed away, allowing for the showdown at high midnight. Maybe we were no better than those shooting the close-ups. Probably not. But history was unfolding nevertheless.

*You must disperse immediately. Now! This is an order. You are subject to arrest or other actions.*

*Fuck the police!*

*You must disperse immediately. Now! This is an order. You are subject to arrest or other actions.*

Again: *Fuck the police!* And again. This soundtrack looped for a few minutes.

Finally, their patience exhausted, the police let it rip. Tear gas cartridges and rubber bullets came flying from the armored vehicles. A white female reporter or blogger or sightseer with a small expensive-looking camera was struck in the stomach, and she knelt on the pavement near us whimpering. The governor had promised earlier that afternoon that authorities would not use tear gas or rubber bullets. Media in the calf pen reported that the canisters were smoke bombs, but they sure smelled like tear gas to me. In the pandemonium, I made out Bob's silhouette across the street, a silver ghost entombed in a cloud of gas.

Pop! There was screaming from the shadows. The guns were out now. A few hundred feet away, some punk shot into the crowd. Matt and I waited a moment to be sure the gunfire had stopped before running toward the corner, just in time to see a limp body being tossed into the back of a car and whisked away. Calm and steady, the police held their fire.

Their armored vehicles began rumbling toward the mob, toward us, toward the violence. I called Bob on the cell phone. He was lost somewhere amid the smoke and shouting. Let's back the fuck out of here, now! Meet us at the truck.

. . .

We made it back to the hotel in time to catch the bartender wiping up. It was a bizarre juxtaposition. The charred and shattered shopping district of West Florissant and the crimson-tiled reflecting pool of the Four Seasons. The black desperation at street level and the noble undertaking of white civilization far above it, tastefully decorated in chromium and hardwoods. The bartender, a young black man, noticing our dishevelment and wild eyes, gave a knowing nod.

What'll you have, gentlemen?

Let me get a gin and juice, bartender. Make it a double.

On the house, he said, sliding the highball my way. Messed up out there, huh?

That ain't the half of it.

Tell the world what you saw here, he said in a whisper. Tell them black lives matter.

Black lives matter. It was the first time I remember having heard the phrase. And I instantly understood what it meant. Equal treatment and equal justice. Nothing less. Nothing more. What was there to debate about that? The great American ideal. Black Lives Matter. It was the first time I'd heard it, but not the last. Certainly, not the last.

# Fade to Black

After the botched springtime execution of a black man in Oklahoma, questions about the humaneness and racial equity of capital punishment were in the news. The next person in the United States scheduled to die was Willie Trottie, a black man who had murdered his common-law wife and her brother. I visited Trottie on death row at the Texas State Penitentiary at Huntsville and filed a report a few months before the Ferguson riot erupted.

In a strange bit of meaningful coincidence, Trottie typed his appraisal of my story from his prison cell on the very night of Michael Brown's killing. The envelope was stamped with pictures of Christmas wreaths and the caption "Joy to the World." I received his correspondence after I had returned from Missouri.

Long letter short: Trottie was not happy with the piece, calling it biased and unfair.

*You being my FIRST interview,* he wrote, *I should not have*

*expected much from the "media," or rather "PRO-DEATH"*
*reporters . . .*

Everyone is a media critic nowadays, I supposed.

Trottie's letter was sad and deflating. Even though his case was open and shut—he'd admitted to murdering two people and shooting two others—he characterized his homicidal rampage as a crime of passion rather than one of premeditated murder. And premeditation is a prerequisite for the death chamber. Trottie argued in his letter that his court-appointed attorney did not—and did not allow him—to make this important distinction to the jury.

It wasn't justice that the system was seeking, Trottie argued. It was the quick and easy death of a black man.

I didn't buy his legal distinction when I'd met him then and I wasn't buying it now. But what would it have hurt to let the man make his case to the jury? Every American is entitled to that.

Trottie seemed equally perturbed by the claim of his former sister-in-common-law that he had written her from prison asking that she place money in his commissary account so that he might purchase snack cakes and skin lotions.

*She was lying out her teeth,* penned Trottie, ever the jailhouse lawyer. *I'm sure she retained those letters as proof?*


Willie Trottie was pronounced dead at 6:35 p.m. on September 10, 2014—twenty-two minutes after receiving a lethal injection of phenobarbital. His last words were: *I'm going home, going to be with the Lord. Find it in your hearts to forgive me. I'm sorry.*

He closed his eyes, then his mouth, and then he moved no more. His sister-in-common-law was in attendance. She said she did not—and never would—forgive Trottie. And she had never bothered to keep his letters.

*Snack cakes notwithstanding, Trottie's complaints about the unjustness of the death-sentencing process and the timing of his letter reminded me what I had been told by Roland Burrow, a soft-spoken black man who was part of the protests in Ferguson.*

*Burrow said that from his perspective, the black community of St. Louis would accept a grand jury's decision not to indict the white officer who had killed the unarmed black teenager if the process was perceived as "fair."*

*But what was fair about a teenager dying at the hands of a police officer when he was carrying no weapon? Burrow asked. That could not be worthy of a death sentence, he said.*

*It is exceedingly rare for a police officer to be charged with the use of deadly force in the United States. Over the previous decade, according to a* Washington Post *analysis, in more than three thousand cases of "death by cop," fifty-four officers had been charged for killing someone in the line of duty, and just eleven of those cases ended in a conviction. In two-thirds of those cases, a white officer shot and killed a black person. In none of those cases did a black officer fatally shoot a white person.*

*Even when there's video, it's unlikely for a cop to face trial. And in the Brown case, there was no video, making the*

possibility that Officer Wilson would be indicted slim to none. Justified or not.

    With the embers still warm and the smell of gas still fresh, Bur-
rows and I both knew then how this thing would play out in the
courtroom and consequently the streets of middle America. Fair
or not.

# Brown Out

Bad and unpredictable things happen in the whirlpool of a riot. Trapped within its vortex, you act unpredictably, skittish, cowardly. No one wants to face his mortality and he tries to avoid it. But if you're a reporter in modern America, civil disturbance is going to find you—a shoot 'em up, a beat 'em down, a take 'em out—that is, if you're any kind of a street reporter.

Back in Ferguson now, I could smell the aroma of another riot brewing. A strange, metaphysical, postmodern type of premeditated violence percolating through the streets. The authorities were everywhere, but unseen, plotting in conference rooms and precinct houses, only to emerge at predetermined times to announce to the media their plans for manpower and response scenarios and to detail their "encouraging" meetings with community activists about peaceful demonstrations.

Michael Brown had been killed three months earlier, but the

Ferguson liquor stores and hair-weave shops had still not replaced their shattered windows. Everything was covered in particle board, and every business owner was figuring on more mayhem to come. At Sam's Meat Market & More, they even hung posters—"Hands Up, Don't Shoot"—to demonstrate solidarity with the black community, seemingly willing to let bygones be bygones.

A grand jury was expected any day now . . . any day now . . . any day now . . . to announce whether Darren Wilson, the white Ferguson police officer, would be charged with murder or manslaughter—or nothing at all—in the case of the shooting of the unarmed Brown.

The hotels and motels were stuffed full with the entire spectrum of the journalism universe: the scabby war photographer; the aim-to-please kid fresh from liberal arts college; the asshole network guy screaming because the coffee pot in the lobby had gone cold; and TV reporters sent in from small markets around the country, who preferred to do their live shots from the motel parking lot, too lazy or scared to go out to the streets where something might actually be happening.

What they would have found had they gone to the streets was the universal expectation that the cop would not be charged: At the beauty salon, the barbershop, the auto-parts store, the apartment complex, the feeling was the same.

You know how it is, said Antoine Drummond, a barber at a West Florissant shop and a father of two. Cops always get off, hands up or not, he said. That's why I say it, man: Fuck the police.

A decision not to charge wasn't going to be popular on the streets of Ferguson, greater St. Louis, or any part of black America for that matter, and so the smart money was on a riot. And each day the grand jury convened, more media flew in with more equipment, overflowing the press conferences that invariably were about nothing much. The media herd needed to be fed.

From the media's point of view, when the decision came, there was going to be some *good TV*. Some flames and gas. Some screaming and looting. Gun sales were brisk. Maybe there would be a cop shooting from either side of the barrel. Makeup tones would be subdued, of course. Wardrobe would tend toward the safari greens and autumnal hiking wear. There could be an Emmy in this, after all. Proper costume could be the difference between winner and first runner-up. Think of it! A local regional Emmy! The sublime trinket of nothingness. The ultimate toilet-roll holder. The fast track to the teleprompter. Fill-in weekend anchor desk, here I come!

And so the media, the bicoastal honey babies, descended on Ferguson, Missouri, in the heart of Middle America. They were out of place here: primped, blown dry, ravenous, pushy, self-important. Mix that with a generous helping of white liberal do-gooders, white anarchists, black nationalists, international commentators, local bloggers, and the new class of do-it-yourself internet Hemingways and you had yourself a genuine, world-class goat fuck of discombobulation and vainglory.

Out on West Florissant Avenue, the technicians from the networks and local stations erected sets along the avenue. They set up behind the iron bars of an abandoned garage and across from Red's BBQ, which had been vandalized twice since Brown's death and hadn't opened since.

There were at least five TV crews, and they were as conspicuous and bothered as baboons' asses in heat. Security personnel, news personalities, support staff, transmission trucks. Again, you could hear the resentment from the barber's chair.

*Man, those motherfuckers are HOPING this shit burns.*

One enterprising crew was setting up early on the roof of a public-storage garage next to Sam's Meat in an attempt to provide a unique aerial advantage to their coverage. Bad idea, I thought, like

smoking in a hayloft. It would be a fifteen-foot jump to the pavement if *They* lit the joint up, if the crew had to escape the flames,
which, no doubt in my mind, they would.

The only thing missing here was a banner stretched across the
street:

## *TV NETWORK NEWS:*
## *FOR ALL YOUR RIOTING NEEDS!*

On the other side of town, near the courthouse in nearby
Clayton, where the grand jury was deliberating, there was a riot
of news vans, trucks, parabolic dishes, electrical wires, klieg lights,
directors' chairs, protective awnings, producers with clipboards,
and reporters—so many reporters, most of them white but a few
of the cappuccino-colored variety, just to keep up the appearance
of diversity on the streets when the cork popped off this stink
bomb.

That's where I saw the Anchorman on his soapbox. He was
smaller and pastier than on TV, decked out in a crisp new parka
with a white fur fringe and the type of multicolored scarf that
elderly women wear—a furry weenie wrapped in polyester and
goose down. The last time I'd seen him was the first time I'd seen
him, maybe ten months earlier in New York City.

Then, I'd gotten intel from a private detective that the president
of the Detroit city council may have been hiding out at the Anchorman's New York apartment. The council president, Charles Pugh
(himself a former local Detroit TV anchorman), had skipped town
in the middle of the night after Bob and I had cornered him at the
city hall elevators and asked if it was true that he was soliciting sex
and sex video from high school boys he "mentored."

That's crazy, Pugh croaked in a queasy, guilt-ridden voice. That's crazy.

It was his last public statement in office.

We staked out the New York apartment building, waiting in our black SUV for Pugh to emerge. Eventually, it was the Anchorman who came down in some sort of housecoat or smoking jacket and an ascot, carrying one of those designer-handbag dogs, which was likewise dressed for the weather. Before you knew it, Bob was out of the truck and in his face with a camera.

What's the meaning of this? the Anchorman fussed.

We have word that Charles Pugh, the former president of the Detroit city council, may be staying with you. Is that true?

And you are? he asked archly.

I gave him my card, then showed off my credentials: NEWS MEDIA PRESS OFFICIAL IDENTIFICATION.

Is Charles Pugh staying with you? Did he visit?

This is outrageous. I don't understand what you're doing here.

Come on, now, I said. You know how it works. I ask the questions, you answer the questions. Then we put your answers on TV. You've seen it a million times. Now, Charles Pugh. Have you seen him?

I promise, if you air this, you will be hearing from my lawyers.

I'll take that as a "no comment," then?

The Anchorman gave an indignant lift of his eyebrow and dialed someone on his phone.

Bob and I walked across the street to the police precinct and hung a handmade wanted poster of Pugh, distributed a few dozen more in the neighborhood, and then we were on our way.

As for Pugh, he eventually pleaded guilty to the repeated rape of a fourteen-year-old "intern" and was sentenced to five to fifteen years in state prison.

· · ·

And so here we met again. The Anchorman in his makeup and parka, standing on his soapbox for his live hit. I stood and watched for a moment . . . he never had answered my question.

Our sources are telling us, he droned, that the grand jury . . . blah, blah, blah.

He was good. Polished. Did not stutter, all the while looking down on me with a peripheral sideways stinkeye. He remembered New York, no doubt.

Me without Bob now. Poor Bob, back in Detroit, recently removed from a ventilator, having nearly died after putting his motorcycle into the rear end of an automobile. I was with Doug, a big, beefy hockey-playing type of white man with a goatee and a Benjamin Franklin hairdo, who had come along from Detroit to double as our producer and bodyguard. Matt was on the phone with engineers back home, trying to figure out satellite booking windows for live shots. Normally Bob would do this, but Bob had scrambled-egg brain. Matt would have to pull all the duties now: photographer, editor, engineer, and—if the shit went down—world-class sprinter. All for the pay of a local news camera guy.

Doug and I walked away from the goat fuck. Farther off now, I continued to peep at the dandy on the soapbox. And the dandy continued to peep at me. And I, him.

Anchorman, please.

Back on West Florissant Avenue in Ferguson, the networks were testing the lights on their impromptu street sets. The crowds were growing. Cars of gawkers and sightseers and looky-loos amassed in the parking lots. The expectation of violence, televised or otherwise, always draws a good audience. We went into Sam's. We were looking for DJ. We were looking for something or someone positive. We didn't find him. Mohammed, a large Arab man, told us he hadn't seen DJ in weeks, since he had come in and asked for a job.

Did you give him one? I asked.

No.

Why? He tried to save your store. You kind of owe him, don't you think?

The Arab shrugged his shoulders, palms up and pleading. Not enough business, he said.

It was a mistake, I thought. In a matter of hours, this place was going to burn if the cop wasn't indicted. A little acknowledgment, a small gesture, something like a part-time job for a black man who protected your livelihood would have gone a long way in this neighborhood.

I wish you luck, I said. Poor mope, he didn't stand a chance.

At least one black man did get a job in all this. Devin James was hired by the white mayor and white chief as a mediator to the black community. James, thirty-two, had everything the white St. Louis establishment was looking for in a black man: He was well spoken (white English) but he also knew the vernacular of the street (black English). He had his own consulting business, but he also had a résumé that included gang-banging, street entrepreneurialism, and homicide.

James was city hall's idea of a young black man living in Ferguson, violent and likely to tear down the town. James could relate. Or as the mayor told me: James brought *a certain perspective.* Shit. James was even shot once and didn't mind removing his shirt to prove it. Hire the man! He killed someone! He brings a certain perspective!

As one of his first orders of business, James convinced Chief Tom Jackson to videotape an apology to the parents of Michael Brown for leaving their son on the baking cement for four hours, his corpse leaking like a sandbag.

This backfired on the streets and at the barbershop, seen by the community both black and white as a disingenuous play for the cameras. Black people asked: Why not tell Brown's parents directly? Why not do it in person? Why do it three months after the fact? Why? people asked. Why apologize at all?

The second pillar of James's strategy was to have the chief join the protesters in a march outside the police station, protesters who were staging a perpetual protest against the chief himself. Predictably (to most), this would not end well. And it did not end well: The chief was pelted with a bag of urine. Two days later, a Ferguson police officer was shot.

So you were protesting yourself? I asked the chief in an interview arranged by James for a profile I was doing about James.

I was just walking, the chief insisted.

No, you were protesting yourself, sir.

The guy was as clueless as the masked white weasel who had grabbed our lens the first time we were here. The chief was bait. Lunch meat. He was going to be swallowed whole by events he could not foresee, by people he did not understand, taking advice from an ex-con with *a certain perspective*.

And as for James, he was let go a few days after our profile of him aired over the eighteen largest local TV markets in the country, including his hometown of Memphis. He was not fired because of the urine dousing or his alligator shoes or his affinity for removing his shirt to show his bullet hole. No, most likely he was dismissed for dancing a jig in the background as I interviewed the chief. Lack of gravitas, or whatever. Two things were obvious about the police in Ferguson.

They didn't have a flipping clue, and they didn't stand a freaking chance.

We drove to the police station on the opposite side of town, parked out back, and waded into the sea of protesters. Matt, who had his one-eye camera, was uncomfortably tethered to Doug by a cable plugged into a portable transmitter. To further burden things, Doug was armed with a selfie stick. We were going to live-stream, a technology we had never used and did not fully understand. When you live-stream, even when you punch pause on the camera, the images continue to upload to the internet in real time. Everything we did and said was there for the world to see, only we didn't realize it.

As we waited for the grand jury's verdict, I spoke to a few groups of young black men from the St. Louis area. To a man, they expressed their frustration and anger in terms of a lack of work. The police harassment. The bogus racial arithmetic: Four black men in a car equals at least one black man spending the evening in jail.

Even if Michael Brown had assaulted the cop, one of them said, even if he had gone for the cop's weapon, even if he had run away, why had he been shot? He was unarmed. Why?

It was a good question. And I didn't have an answer, only questions. Why would you put your hand on a cop? And why do so many young black men kill each other? Don't the killings contribute to the stereotype of a boogeyman?

One young man, wrestling with monumental notions of social economics and equity and self-responsibility, eventually broke it down in terms anyone listening could understand: I don't know. It just ain't fair, man.

It just ain't fair, man.

Stretched above us, spanning the street, the holiday lights glowed: "Season's Greetings," the banner read.

Shortly after 8 p.m., it was announced over a bullhorn: The grand jury would not indict. Blood patterns and some skin from the teenager's thumb in Wilson's car and powder residue on Brown's thumb that was consistent with Wilson's gun having been discharged at very close range supported the cop's story about them struggling with his weapon near the car. At least to the grand jury it seemed realistic. What's more, Brown had not been shot in the back, as his friend had told the world via TV.

Residue. Ballistic testing. Blood spatter. Science be damned. The streets did not want to hear it. To compound the problem, the county prosecutor had inexplicably waited until nightfall to announce the jury's decision. Brown's stepfather stood on the hood of a car outside the Ferguson police station.

Burn this motherfucker down! he shouted. Burn this bitch down!

The crowd took him at his word. The orgy began.

Protesters marched down the street. Left unmolested, they would have ended up out in the dark void of the interstate. But the police inexplicably blocked them off and thus bottled them up in the middle of town. With no place to go, protesters decided to hurl bricks and glass. Gunshots came next. Two police cars were set on fire; the bullets inside the cruisers exploded from the heat.

One of the young men I had spoken to earlier under the holiday lights jumped on a squad car and smashed out the windshield. He recognized me and waved like a friendly neighbor picking up the newspaper off his front porch before loping off into the abyss.

Two women, young and as nicely dressed as secretaries, threw rocks through a plate-glass window, giggling like schoolgirls as it shattered. Matt and Doug, tethered and one-eyed, were pelted with rocks and bits of construction brick as bullets exploded indiscriminately and tear gas blanketed the street. They decided to move off to safety. Locked in the maelstrom, I couldn't find them. When I did, we fought, challenging each other's integrity and honor about leaving a man behind, all while our live stream rolled on as we gagged on tear gas fumes.

Like I said, apparently pushing pause on the camera doesn't pause the live stream. I have never had the heart to watch the video myself, but I believe the word "pussy" and other choice adjectives were exchanged between us. We were brothers, but poor and humiliating things were said in the heat of an agonizing moment.

You can always apologize in the morning. But it made it that much more difficult when you're trending on Facebook.

Up the street, near the relative safety of the police cordon, a network reporter put on his gas mask incorrectly, trapping the stinging smoke inside and accidentally gassing himself on a live broadcast. He squealed for water. He too would be trending by morning. TV's a bitch.

We made our way to West Florissant, where the violence was worse. The whole district, it seemed, was on fire. Gunshots were echoing through the streets, the National Guard was nowhere to be seen, and the firefighters had dropped their hoses and run. Stretched across the avenue, sidewalk to sidewalk, were police in riot gear, much of it ill-fitting, helmets cockeyed and akimbo, misapplied gas masks fogging up from extended use. I felt sorry for these men and women, black and white, a plastic shield the only thing between them and a bullet.

We were leaning against a storefront, when one of the riot police began to shout at me. I could not understand what he said through his steaming mask.

Excuse me, sir?

He shouted again. I moved closer.

Excuse me, sir?

You, he shouted. Are you the guy that made that video on the squatter?

Yes sir.

I just saw it on YouTube. That was fucking hilarious. Outstanding work, sir!

And he took my hand and shook it. It was indeed a strange, postmodern riot.

We inched farther down the street, trying not to get gassed or shot or mugged. Liquor store on fire. AutoZone on fire. Original Red's BBQ on fire. Across the street, the media was long gone, being one of the first things attacked by rioters. Their temporary sets had been trampled and torn and torched. What happened to the camera crew on top of the storage garage? I looked up. The flames were thirty feet high and they were gone. Next to that, Sam's Meat Market & More. On fire. Again. Nothing left but the walls.

I couldn't help but think it: They should have hired DJ.


I went back to the hotel early in the morning, turned on the TV, and lit a smoke. I sat with my lips pressed against the window screen blowing smoke into the dark air already filled with vapor.

The news presenters had accents from the British Empire. The young, light-skinned black guy was from England, was my guess, and the aging white woman from Australia.

The television set was mounted on the wall, creating a relationship where I was looking up at it and it was looking down on me. It gave me a feeling of being infantilized. Mommy and Daddy in my bedroom talking down to me, lecturing, moralizing, haranguing. I wondered how many millions of others were receiving the same "talking to" at that very moment. And like a child, I resented it.

Their set was blue. Their makeup thick. Their clothing immaculate. There was no telling where in the world they were broadcasting from, but it surely wasn't Ferguson. Still, that did not prevent them from commenting on the evening's mayhem as if they had been here, as if they had grown up here and understood the nuances and complexities of American life. What the world heard from them was that this was simply another case of a white cop killing a young, unarmed black man and the looters and arsonists were simply voicing their historical discontentment and here was another case of the abject failure of the American experience.

I watched them and wept.

# 2015

It had been a rough year: We'd suffered a stoning of batteries and a traffic-cone beatdown, two tear gassings, guns pointed in our direction, morose tales of children beaten by smugglers. The mundane desperation of a twenty-dollar blow job seemed to permeate the devolution of the American Way.

We'd smelled the cold, rank odor of corpses in culverts and stared into the dead, disinterested pupils of television executives. We had traveled more than thirty thousand miles through airport toilets, truck stops, fleabag motels, last-chance towns, culminating with a night of self-inflicted humiliation in Ferguson. Suffering from fatigue and mutual bitterness, we needed a break from the road.

Ferguson was an important place with its majority black population led by a tone-deaf and greedy bureaucracy of whites. But Ferguson was just a small town. Detroit, the gargantuan city of dysfunction, was the big American story. Having emerged from bankruptcy, Motown had a new mayor—a white man—who had been in office for a year.

People wanted to believe this man was the Great White Hope,

*someone fresh and clean. I was skeptical. After all, jobbery, double-talk, and connivance are the skills required to assume and keep the seat of power in an industrial city with a long history of corruption.*

*Consider Coleman A. Young. Detroit's first black mayor, a towering and divisive figure. He is credited by blacks with integrating the police force and placing African Americans in positions of power. He is credited by whites, on the other hand, with having quickened the city's decline and therefore their forced exodus to the suburbs. But Young was also cozy with the wealthy white business elite and allowed them to gouge the public coffers. He was also the near-perpetual subject of federal corruption probes.*

*The following quotation about duplicity and race is a rare moment of honesty from a politician. The honesty, however, was accidental, since Young did not know he was being audiotaped by an associate of his wearing a wire, having turned informant for the FBI.*

*"We'd have politicians come by, make speeches. We'd hire some winos and shit, you know, and they'd line up and listen . . . and [we'd] just load them in cars, the same motherfuckers . . . and we'd take advantage of racism, see? Because they figured that all black folks looked alike, they couldn't tell the difference. They might make four speeches to the same group of people. That's sad, see. I've done that myself."*

*Young confirmed that what you see in politics is not what you get, but people aren't smart enough to notice. Especially media.*

*Today, the skin color and turns of phrase may have changed in city hall, but reading Young's words, I'm reminded that if history doesn't have a way of repeating itself, it at least has a way of stuttering.*

# Ebony & Ivory

**DETROIT (WINTER)—**

The first time I'd met Mike Duggan, in 2013, he was running for mayor of Detroit. If elected, he would be the first white man to occupy the chair in four decades. But the sledding would not be easy. An early front-runner, he had been kicked off the ballot because he hadn't lived in the city long enough, having moved from Livonia (the whitest city in Michigan) to Detroit (the blackest) less than a year before.

As a carpetbagger, he was nevertheless allowed to run as a write-in candidate in the nonpartisan primary, a seemingly impossible proposition in a city where half the adult population was said to be functionally illiterate.

Duggan, a Democrat, wasn't only facing the issue of poor spelling; he was staring down the barrel of a tradition of Detroit political shenanigans dating back a century. I wrote an online-only column about past attempts to muddy the election waters by fielding candidates whose names were similar or identical to that of the incumbent. I remarked that given the city's well-chronicled penchant for creative campaigning, I wouldn't be shocked to see another Mike Duggan or Mike Doogan or Miles Dillon suddenly jump into the mix to confuse voters, siphon votes away, or cause them to be tossed out altogether due to misspellings.

Lo and behold, about a week later, I received an early-morning call from a politically connected acquaintance who informed me that there was indeed such a character preparing to throw his hat in the ring as a write-in candidate. The primary was less than two weeks away.

It's a good story, the caller said. You should get on this right away, before any of your competitors do.

I was given the straw man's address, and Bob and I dutifully drove to the West Side neighborhood and knocked on the door of the crumbling Tudor of Mike Dugeon, a young black barber.

Mike the Black, bleary-eyed and half dressed, seemed genuinely confounded. He assured us he had no idea what we were talking about. He denied he'd been contacted by any campaign or union boss.

I tried to explain the whole shebang to him, the political chess, the matter of misspelling. If voters couldn't write Mike the White Man's name properly, who's to say they weren't trying to write Mike the Black Man's name properly? D-U-G-G-A-N. D-U-G-E-O-N. Everything would be in disarray. The more Mike the Black thought about this, the more he warmed to the idea.

We need someone to talk about what's going on in the 'hood, he said to me, fully a year before places like Ferguson and Baltimore would explode in unfocused fury. Maybe this way, if I'm running for mayor, he continued, They'll listen to Us. Besides, he would later confide, there could be free publicity for him if he got in, more customers at the barbershop, maybe even a reality TV show.

So Mike the Black excused himself for a moment, went upstairs and dressed, then drove to city hall to exercise his constitutional rights. Bob and I followed.

Mike the Black had no realistic shot, and he knew it. He'd never so much as run for student body council. He had never cast a vote in his life, for that matter. But he was a fresh face from the neighborhood, a young black face who understood the problems of crime and unemployment and boredom. He was also, in true American campaign style, promising free Subway sandwiches, chips, and pop for every citizen. So one never really knew.

Mysteriously, when Mike the Black arrived at the city clerk's office, the woman behind the counter was waiting with all the necessary paperwork, as if she'd been expecting him. More mysterious, when the barber was told he would need to go across town to have the papers notarized at a separate government office, the notary from *that separate government office* waltzed in and breezily signed off on his forms. Most mysterious, within minutes of his filing his papers, a "Dugeon for Detroit" Facebook page popped up out of nowhere, its colors and logos almost identical to Mike the White's campaign literature "Duggan for Detroit." The calls started coming in to the barber almost immediately that afternoon from reporters and politicos alike. Mike the Black wondered how they'd gotten his number. It was weird.

Some local journalists were eager to blame me for trying to swing the primary, as if I'd orchestrated the whole affair. A second theory among them was that the barber was in fact in the pocket of some nefarious cabal—namely, Duggan's opposition. Rumors began swirling. Dugeon, some noted, was the hairstylist to the brother-in-law of one of the other leading candidates.

Nobody, it should be said, supposed Mike the Black had done it on his own.

Puffed-up and pear-bottomed reporters spoke in concerned baritones, as if they had never seen anything so outrageous in all their years in the news business. Detroit had officially filed for bankruptcy just the week before. Things were teetering on the edge in the Motor City. This election, they opined, was *serious business.* And now someone was manipulating the process, making the city a mockery and a laughingstock. Even the simplest things in Detroit could not be done on the level.

Trouble brewing, I made a call to Mike the White's representatives, who made him available for a late-afternoon interview at his new Detroit residence, the home that had started all this trouble.

Mike the White met us in the circular driveway. He was gracious enough. He did not blame me for this outrage. Instead, he blamed his main opponent, Wayne County sheriff Benny Napoleon. It was obvious who had put the barber up to it, Mike the White told our viewing audience. It was plain as the nose on his face who had set the day's events in motion. It was the sheriff in a despicable display of dirty politics, he complained.

This of course was horseshit, because it had been Duggan's man who had called me that morning with the "tip" that set the day's events in motion. It was Duggan's man who gave me the barber's address, explaining that they'd gotten the name and the game plan from a mole inside the sheriff's campaign.

Looking back, I can only think . . . maybe. Maybe Napoleon's people were contemplating such a maneuver and an inside mole had leaked this information to Duggan. Or maybe the mole was actually a double agent whose job was to feed Duggan false information to trip him up. Or just maybe there was no mole at all and I was given a false tip by Duggan's man in the hope that I would cobble together an unflattering story about Napoleon while simultaneously getting the proper spelling of his boss's name into the news. D-U-G-G-A-N.

I called Napoleon. He insisted he never had a plan in the works. Maybe. The barber too had already claimed ignorance of any Napoleon connection. Again, maybe.

What I do know is that Duggan stood bald-faced in front of our camera and spat out some wooden-nickel narrative implying that his camp had nothing to do with it. And that spoke volumes about the man's character. It confirmed for me yet again that no matter how you slice the shit sandwich of politics, you're still eating shit.

Whatever the true genesis of Mike the Black's entry into the race, Mike the White hammered on the story hard. He got his headlines. There were radio jingles, graffiti all around town on the abandoned houses and storefronts.

D-U-G-G-A-N. The little white man running for the city's biggest office even rolled up his sleeves and scrubbed the graffiti from the buildings, but only when a camera was around.

I felt I'd been played. The barber felt he'd been played. And worse, the barber believed, to some extent, that I had played him, encouraging him to jump in headfirst. And maybe I did. I didn't twist his arm, but I had been the one who had knocked on his door, woke him from his morning slumber, and explained the scenarios to him.

In my defense, without that phone call from Duggan's man, I never would have found my way to Dugeon's porch. But once I was there, I wasn't leaving until he'd made a decision. I needed an answer. I'm media, remember? Scum. TV.

But Mike the Black jumped without realizing he was leaping headfirst into a one-foot concrete pool. He was a mouse in a meat grinder. The media jackals kept yipping, pawing, ridiculing him over the next days as a dupe and a dope and a tool of the political machine—or, worse, the stooge of a TV reporter. His dreams of stardom dissolved into a nightmare of public humiliation. So the barber went into hiding, shattered, demoralized, afraid of the shadowy people calling him with offers to stay in the race and others to get out of the race.

In the end, Mike Duggan won the mayor's office in an improbable multi-million-dollar write-in campaign. He then turned around and flipped his new Detroit house for a neat 20 percent profit and moved into the mayor's mansion. At least that's what he told the press. Nobody ever checked to see if he and his family had actually moved there.

As for Mike Dugeon? He got carjacked at gunpoint.

A nd so I met Duggan for the second time, a year after he had assumed office. To that point, his responsibilities had been light, considering the bankrupt city had been under the authority of a state-appointed emergency manager and had only recently emerged from Chapter 9 and been turned over to civilian control. But that didn't stop Hizzoner from taking credit for a raft of accomplishments that were either untrue or not of his doing. Streetlights were coming back on. (True.) The budget was balanced. (True.) Crime was down. (Unclear.) The population flight had stopped as white people were moving back in. (False.)

At our lunch date, Duggan appeared wrinkled and beet red, like a man being wheeled through the hospital with chest pain. The remaining strands of his hair were poorly combed. His jacket was shabby and unpressed, the necktie frayed at the knot. His left shoelace was untied. There was something artful and cunning in the disheveled manner of his habiliments, I thought. Played down and unremarkable, like his choice of this empty restaurant. A vacant second floor above a bar, except for the officer in the corner and a solitary waiter, hands folded at the ready.

Politics—Duggan's politics—were a poker match. The more concealed, the greater your chances.

Here was a man the public knew very little of despite his being a Democratic high roller for thirty years. The machine head. Party boss. A man whose name half the town mispronounced despite the jingles.

Chicken noodle soup and a chicken wrap, ordered the mayor without looking at the waiter. And an iced tea, light on the ice.

Understated, I thought. Noncommittal. Good play. I'll see your chicken soup and chicken wrap. And I'll raise with a coffee please, cream, real cream, none of that fake shit in a sealed thimble.

The waiter nodded and disappeared.

Duggan had mentioned a story of mine in his State of the City speech a few evenings before, one where I had answered a run-of-the-mill Detroit home invasion call and waited with the woman as she waited on the police to arrive. I was able to go to McDonald's twice, take a bubble bath, pad around her home in a bathrobe (Matt unnecessarily pixelated my balls in postproduction), read her grandchildren a bedtime story, and, four hours later, still had to walk out on the lawn and wave down a passing cruiser.

Gone are those days, the mayor proclaimed in his speech.

It was political sleight of hand. I knew it. He knew it. The police knew it. The whole way the bankruptcy was sold to the citizens was to loosen up money for public safety. But where did the money go? Police, their pensions and salaries cut, were leaving in droves. And where were the results? The murder rate was the same, more or less, with Detroit hovering in its customary place among the bloodiest cities in the country. It was still the most violent city in America. Arrests were way down. And the crime numbers appeared cooked. But if no one checks the lie, the lie becomes the truth.

It wasn't getting caught in speechifying hyperbole that was the primary weakness of his administration, however; it was his whiteness, or so he seemed to think.

Young white people were moving in, and that was a good thing. These fresh-faced trailblazers didn't need much. Cocooned in the downtown silk-stocking district, they did not particularly need municipal infrastructure like police and schools or affordable insurance. After all, they had no children and they could register their cars at their parents' homes in the 'burbs. And when they did need schools for their children, they would be gone to the 'burbs again.

But these were basics that black people living in the neighborhoods had done without for years. Now, as public investment funneled through billionaire developers poured into the downtown area while their blocks continued to crumble, the grumblings from the neighborhoods became as continual as a drumbeat.

We've got to maintain the return of young white professionals, Duggan said. But we need to get the young black professionals back too. Detroit's been losing population for six decades. Ultimately, that's how I should be judged. If the city starts to grow in population.

He needed young black professionals to front this story of a New Detroit, however few there may have been, otherwise the narrative of a renaissance would not fly in a city that was more than 80 percent black. And to that effect, Duggan hired black people and sent them out in front of the cameras and to the neighborhood meetings, preferring, whenever possible, he said in not so many words, to keep his whiteness tempered. He preferred ribbon cuttings and dog pound openings to handshaking and baby hugging.

They know you're white, I said to him. They voted for you anyway. White people voted for Obama. What's the problem?

It's best to let the young people do the talking, he said. Then he wiped his lips and set his napkin on the table.

Lunch finished, the reluctantly white mayor excused himself, saying he had much to do. Back to the eleventh floor, the dark hardwood desk, the big chair, the heavy crown. With the whole pitch about revitalization, he almost had me believing.

As I left, however, I couldn't help thinking back to Mike Dugeon, the barber from the neighborhood. No one had offered him a job in politics since the day he'd decided to wade into the shark-infested waters of the mayor's race. He was probably too disgusted with the government and the media anyway. Last I heard, he had reemerged as a Black Hebrew and was now proselytizing in the streets.

*Rested and roused by my luncheon with the unwilling white mayor, I was back on the American road of insanity, on my way to Alabama in search of another unwilling white man who had apparently withdrawn himself from history.*

*He had been a cop in Birmingham during the civil rights era. He was famous not for his name, but for his photographic image. On the plane trip down to find him, I was reading up on the history of that time. The following words are from a letter penned by Reverend Dr. Martin Luther King Jr. while he was locked up in the Birmingham city jail in April 1963.*

*Known as "The Negro Is Your Brother," the letter is addressed to Southern white clergymen who had denounced the civil rights tactics. King's letter defends the strategy of nonviolent disobedience in the face of racism and mocks the white ministers' praise for the Birmingham police for keeping order.*

*"I doubt that you would have so warmly commended the police force if you had seen its dogs sinking their teeth into unarmed, nonviolent Negroes," Dr. King wrote.*

*It seemed as though his letter was written specifically about the man I had come looking for. And it very well may have been.*

# Yellowhammer

A young white woman was setting strudel on the racks to cool. Two Latinos were kneading dough in the threshold of the kitchen. A good old girl emerged from the toilet. It was not Dick.

The cuckoo clock barked ten. *Cuckoo! Cuckoo! Cuckoo! Cuckoo!* . . . The door front opened. The bell tinkled. Again, an old white woman, pale and silver. Again, not Dick.

Wherever Dick Middleton was this morning, it was easy to see he appreciated German things. A German bakery in the suburbs of Birmingham. A German wife whom he met while serving in Germany after the war. The German cuckoo clocks. And you might remember Dick's old dog Leo, the German shepherd from that photograph taken back in '63.

It was and is still an important picture. The clench-jawed Officer Middleton, his white nostrils flared, his crisp peaked cap with the patent-leather visor adorned with a silver eagle, the silver sunglasses, the leather holster on his left hip. The picture of authority straining with the leash of Leo with his left hand as the dog lunges into the belly of a black teenager. Officer Middleton snatching at the teen's sweater with his right hand. There is something Germanic to this scene, something despotic and dictatorial. Power conceding nothing. *The Man.*

*The Boy*, Walter Gadsden, fifteen, was playing hooky from school that day to watch the goings-on. Dressed in a cardigan, his pants pocket turned inside out. His left hand clenched around the right wrist of Officer Middleton, either in defiance or to steady himself as Leo tore into him. Onlookers appeared shocked, aggravated, each looking over his shoulder at the scene as he scurries away, wanting no trouble. Gadsden's face was pensive yet calm, revealing nothing, no fear, no shock, no rage. The marquee of a diner above the boy's head reads:

**JOCKEY BOY**
**RESTAURANT**
**DRINK**
*Coca-Cola*

Without this black-and-white photograph there would probably be no Civil Rights Act, no Voting Rights Act, nor any sort of equal rights act at all. There certainly would have been no "Bloody Sunday" march in Selma, an event whose fiftieth anniversary was being marked by a Hollywood film playing in theaters across the country. It was this image of the cop and the dog and the boy—snapped in Birmingham two years before Bloody Sunday—that brought the question of American apartheid to a head.

In early 1963, Martin Luther King Jr. and the movement he led were in jail and stuck in the mud. They could claim few victories in Alabama since Rosa Parks had inspired the Montgomery Bus Boycott eight years earlier. They needed something. So two weeks after writing the letter from the Birmingham jail, King and his Southern Christian Leadership Conference sent three thousand black schoolchildren into the streets to protest segregation and all the shit that went with it.

In response, Birmingham commissioner of public safety Eugene "Bull" Connor unleashed police dogs and fire hoses and Dick Middleton, and ordered the mass arrest of the children. Associated Press photographer Bill Hudson was there with his camera.

The photograph of the boy being set upon by a snarling dog ran on nearly every front page in America (though not in Birmingham). President John F. Kennedy said it made him sick.

From that point, history unfolded. Desegregation in Birmingham. The bombing just months later of the city's 16th Street Baptist Church by the Ku Klux Klan, killing four young schoolgirls. The Civil Rights Act. The Selma march. The Voting Rights Act. The assassination of King.

For years, the men in the picture—the scene is also immortalized in a bronze statue in a park in the center of Birmingham—remained nearly anonymous. The fifteen-year-old boy, Walter Gadsden, was reached three decades later by Pulitzer Prize-winning historian Diane McWhorter. Their conversation was short, McWhorter told me when I reached her by telephone in New York City. Gadsden had told her that he didn't want to "become involved" and politely hung up the phone.

The Birmingham police officer, identified by McWhorter and his former colleagues in the police department as Dick Middleton, told McWhorter that the photograph "didn't bother me."

Black teen, white cop, brutality—more than fifty years later, it was still the stuff of headlines. I believed the two men might have more to offer history than two short phone interviews. And with the TV circus sure to be descending on the Edmund Pettus Bridge in Selma next week to photograph President Obama walking arm in arm with the black protesters who were savaged then by police, it would be a historic moment, no doubt. But it would be a picture taken by a thousand media types, uninspired and uninteresting. So I decided to avoid it altogether.

When the media turns right, always go left. Like Jimmy Breslin, the great New York reporter, said, everybody goes to the winners' locker room. Breslin always went to find the losers. I went to find Walter, the boy frozen in time, and Dick, the eternal face of oppression, hoping they were still alive, hoping they had something to say. Some explanation. Something about the state of things now. Some way forward.

I searched the public records nationwide but found no evidence of a Walter Gadsden having died. He did seem to have vanished into history, however. I found no voter registration. No next of kin. No contacts with historians or civil rights groups.

I was able to whittle the choices down to three Walter Gadsdens, all living in Alabama, according to the records. The first lived in a cheerless apartment block next to the road leading out of Birmingham, situated on a cement berm. There was a half-smoked butt on the windowsill next to the door. Bedsheets covered the windows. I knocked three times. A young black man eventually answered. I showed him the photograph.

Wrong dude, he said, closing his door, going back to his business.

The second Walter Gadsden lived in Montgomery.

I don't know nothing 'bout no dog, his daughter told me over the phone. Besides, he ain't old enough. I'm sorry, she said before kindly excusing herself.

The third was an address on the east side of Birmingham, on the other side of some railroad tracks. There was a burned-down barbecue joint next to the Gadsden home and a stand of trees on the other side, in a glen littered with barrels and bottles, where the yellowhammers crowed with a violence.

With Bob behind me rolling tape, I peeled back some broken security bars, slid my hand through a ripped screen, and knocked on the door. An old, thin, gummy black man answered. His hair was gray and untended, his shirt the consistency of a used nose rag. He screamed poverty, but there was self-regard in the uprightness of his manners, something distinguished. It aroused an admiration in me and I wanted to express my respect in some way, an acknowledgment of his years and ability to survive. I could make out a silent, oversized television set in the cluttered living room and a fish tank gone green with neglect. You could hear a woman screaming at him from a cell phone in his pocket.

I reached out and gave him my hand.

You're not here to knock my head in, is you? he said before reaching out and accepting me.

I showed him the photograph.

I remember it. My gracious, that policeman look mean, I must say.

What about the kid? Is that you?

No, not me, he said, wheezing like an oboe. But I was there.

My spirit flagged. I knew then I would never find the Walter Gadsden of 1963.

Has anything changed? I asked lamely after some disappointed silence.

Yes, a lot has changed, the man said. And then again, not a whole lot has changed. Not a whole lot. We can eat in restaurants and so forth. But police is still beating on young black men. Not enough has changed, not a whole lot when you really get down to it.

The afternoon was cold and gray and mean. The neighborhood was no better. There were bars over every street-level window on every street for three blocks all the way to the railroad tracks. Porches falling in. Vehicles that hadn't moved in years. There were no people about. The leaves alone moved in the wind.

The woman on the phone in the man's pocket was still screaming, lathered up, cussing him out: *You no-good so-and-so, you lying piece of what-not, who you talking to? You there, hello? You listening to me?*

The old man, smiling with a dignified embarrassment, excused himself and closed the door, leaving us alone on his porch with the shrieking of the yellowhammers.

B ob shrugged his shoulders. He was back from his near-death experience on the motorcycle. Unsteady, but back neverthe-less, and I was glad to have him. I too love German things. Bob Schedlbower. Bob the Skull Farmer, in the English translation. Matt was back in Detroit holding out for a raise; having been shelled in Ferguson, having been peppered with rocks and bricks and tear gas, he wanted a little acknowledgment. A dollar-an-hour "atta boy" from management. Matt Phillips. Matt the Lover of Horses, in translation. Bob and Matt, the offspring of cabbage farmers and stable hands. The descendants of peasants.

B ob and I drove way out into the Alabama countryside of Tal-ladega County to the home of Nolen Shivers, a forty-nine-year veteran with the Birmingham Police Department. Shivers, who was assigned to the jail that week in 1963, said he had booked hundreds of people—and was one of two who would have taken King's finger-prints and mug shot. I was sick with the flu, and before we made the final bend to Shivers's place, I had to jump out of the car and relieve myself. Despite appearances, TV can be an ugly and unglamorous beast. Good thing we brought extra napkins along from Dick's bakery.

Shivers's home was the inverse of the Gadsden place back in Bir-mingham; it was tasteful and clean with a wide fishing lake in the back. The quiet chirping of whippoorwills. No screaming woman or woodpeckers here, no sir.

Shivers looked me up and down, pale and feverish. He went to the kitchen and poured me a vodka and soda pop to settle my stom-ach before settling his attention on the photograph. "It is 5 o'clock somewhere," the sign above his kitchen threshold read.

Cocktail in hand, Shivers explained that his job was to book and fingerprint those arrested during the week. Hundreds, maybe a thousand, no telling. Back then, he continued, King wasn't known that well, but he was arrested along with the group. It may have been him who'd taken King's prints.

You know the officer in the photo?

Yes, that's Dick Middleton.

You sure?

Yeah.

You worked with him?

I knew Middleton, and I wrote his name down many times in the docket books where he had made an arrest. He worked canine. Look at his holster. On the left hip. Dick was left-handed.

They had worked together for twenty years, and I asked Shivers about those times, his lawman's role in maintaining segregation, his participation in the booking and locking up of hundreds of chil-dren, King's letter written from his jailhouse.

In my eye, I done nothing wrong while I was working, he said. I was just doing a job. We all were. I knew things was changing and I'm glad they did. It wasn't right. A black person traveling across the country, and couldn't use the bathroom. It's time had come. But yeah, that is Officer Middleton.

A wave of nausea overwhelmed me. I ran to his toilet and vomited. Looking around, I marveled at the cleanliness of the widower's toilet. The clean lip of the bowl. The fresh hand towels. This was a man of orderliness. When I came back to his living room, he had refreshed my drink.

I admire your work ethic, he said.

M iddleton's voter registration listed two addresses. One had led us to the cuckoo-clock bakery. The other to a house in suburban Birmingham. If Middleton had been black, that disparity would have no doubt been enough to make him ineligible to vote back in the days of the Jim Crow South when simply being born out of wedlock was enough to steal a man's right to vote. I had called his house numerous times. I left messages. He never called back.

A reporter's questions of apartheid and attack dogs tend to make strudel taste funny—so Bob and I left the bakery without a word, not wanting to cause upset. Driving around looking for Middleton's home, we passed an abandoned strip mall where the clock had stopped some unknown time ago at 4:14. I was reminded of the famous Bible passage.

*Whereas ye know not what shall be on the morrow. For what is*
*your life? It is even a vapor, that appeareth for a little time, and*
*then vanisheth away.*

*—James 4:14*

Dick lived in a well-appointed subdivision with tasteful land-
scaping and the occasional lawn jockey. (White, mind you! My how
times have changed, yes indeedy!) We parked at the top of the driveway after clipping a decorative boulder near the mailbox and walked
down the sloping driveway to his front door. A dog yipped from
inside the house, and a meaty-faced, middle-aged white man eventually opened up. He was Middleton's son-in-law, he said. I asked
for Dick.

He's not here.

I showed the son-in-law the photograph of Middleton clutching Leo.

It's not him, the son-in-law said, too quickly and rather uncon-
vincingly.

There was only one police officer in the Birmingham department named Dick Middleton and the son-in-law confirmed that his
Dick was in fact a cop in the department. He also said I wasn't the
first to make the mistake. Others had brought the photograph to
the door before and been told the same. It was not his Dick.

Maybe I could come back and ask him?

Oh, he's here.

Can I speak to him?

No.

After twenty years in journalism, not much surprised me anymore. But I must say, I was stunned standing there in Birmingham,
Alabama. Dick Middleton has gone down in history as one of the
faces of white persecution, but neither he nor his family had anything to say about it. He was not home and then he was home. No
explanation, no interpretation, not even an "I was just following
orders" wave of the hand. Just a tepid denial that it was him at all.

I reminded the son-in-law about Dick's phone interview with
McWhorter, the historian, where he confirmed it was indeed

him in the picture. I told him about the recollection of Shivers, Middleton's longtime coworker. And the newspaper clippings
over the years. This was certainly his father-in-law in the photograph? No?

No.

And with that he gently closed the door on history.

Dick Middleton would die later in the year, the unwilling white
man, a vapor who appeared for a short time and then vanished.

The photograph, however . . . the photograph lives forever.

*Iowa rarely makes the national news unless there's a natural disaster or a mass shooting. When it does, you know the political season is upon us. I always had my misgivings about covering the political class's highly orchestrated—and completely deadening—campaign choreography.*

*But with things unraveling across the country, and looking for a juxtaposition, I figured it might be worthwhile to check out the Iowa presidential shitshow, if only to see if any of the candidates had any clue as to what was really going on in real-life America.*

*A dozen Republican hopefuls and Hillary Clinton were invited to field questions from an agricultural magnate who'd struck it rich on corn and pork bellies.*

*I knew a couple things about national politicians. For one, they are primped and prissy, pampering themselves on the taxpayers' dime, but go to great lengths to disguise this fact. (Even their haircuts and manicures are subsidized by the public, the senators' barbershop requiring a half-million-dollar bailout.) That's how it goes in Washington, where you can't see your representative as he really exists.*

*On the campaign trail, however, he rolls up his sleeves, eats chicken on a stick, and tells you with feigned disgust that people like him should be tossed in the stockade.*

*Another thing I knew about national politics was that Iowa votes first in the presidential primaries, giving the agricultural*

*Hawkeye State an unreasonable and oversized influence on the national election. Technically, Iowans hold a freak show known as a "caucus," which means groups of white people standing around screaming at one another for hours before finally being allowed to vote.*

*Lewis Carroll described a similar scene in* Alice in Wonderland. *Alice and the animals meet at the riverbank of tears to discuss how best to dry off. The dodo bird suggests holding a caucus race whereby every creature begins running in a circle until told to stop. This gives rise to no clear winner.*

*In Iowa, they simply gave us Senator Ted Cruz.*

# Red Meat

I ran into Senator Ted Cruz, the Texas Republican, at the Agriculture Summit in Des Moines. More exact, Texas Ted ran into me. He made a beeline, in fact. Ted likes the camera. He feeds off it. His slender shoulders seem to widen, his chest expands, his eyes narrow into thoughtful repose whenever one is around.

He'd interrupted my cigarette, but I pride myself on preparation, and quickly mustered a question about his views on immigration. He said he was pretty much against it. He wanted the border zipped up and a concrete fence erected—making him the first candidate I'd heard of to propose a great wall along the Mexican border. Furthermore, he did not support any road to citizenship for those who had sneaked into the United States of America. Period.

I am the son of an immigrant who came fifty-eight years ago from Cuba—came legally, Cruz emphasized as we stood out in the chilly parking lot of the state fairgrounds. And I think Americans are agreed that amnesty is wrong, he added.

Cruz was wearing a tie and no jacket. Midwesterners love a guy who takes his jacket off. Makes him look like he knows what he's doing.

Cruz was shorter than I'd expected, with a tablespoon too much hair product and a suit wrinkled by miles on the cabbage patch stump. The race for the White House had already begun and we were still a year and three-quarters out from election day. But this wasn't even Cruz's first trip to Iowa or his second. By my unofficial count, he had made more trips to the Hawkeye State than to the Texas border since becoming the Lone Star State's junior senator two years prior. Forget the women and children flooding in from Central America. If you wanted to be president, you had to be in Iowa.

That was the conventional political wisdom, anyway. But I wasn't so sure. The nexus of politicos and media pundits, however, had a stranglehold on the process. They controlled the message, the location, and the rhythms, thereby creating the blandest, most poorly rated, most expensive reality show in the world. Agricultural Summit, ladies and gentlemen. Ethanol credits! Manure retention ponds!

Out there in America they were talking about war and retirement, the workingman who was resorting to turning his underpants inside out to get twice as much use out of them. Regular people were talking about the jobs going to foreign lands and the foreigners coming here to compete for what was left. The inexorable swirl to the bottom. But never mind them. We're talking compensation to retire farming acreage here!

According to the press handout, there were more than 250 media outlets at the summit. With nothing to do, no stories to tell from the state fairgrounds parking lot, they saw that I had Big Ted on the hook, and they swarmed like fish flies. Ted wasn't saying much, something about getting back to the values of the Iowa farmer. I had no idea what he was talking about, but a Japanese reporter shook her head appreciatively.

Yes, thank you, Mr. Senator. *Domo arigato.*

Iowa, by virtue of being the first state to hold a caucus, got the attention first. As far as I could see, the whole show needed to be canceled. But it would roll on for months with a stale energy of its own. I felt sorry for the political press who seemed unaware that their souls were becoming calcified.

Ted went on, puffing like a blowfish at the magnification of attention being paid him: If we allow people who came here illegally to be put on a path to citizenship, that is incredibly unfair to those who follow the rules, he opined.

Biscuits like that had helped make the senator a Tea Party darling and the bus driver of the far-right express. He was a Latino whose stump speech about his father's "legal" path to the American dream was by now a well-polished plum that recounted a Tony Montana–esque journey from Cuban political prisoner (the old man had actually fought *alongside* Fidel Castro) to Texas dishwasher to Canadian oilman to American evangelical pastor.

Indeed, Cruz's immigration stance was a tough yet hypocritical one from a guy taking big money from Wall Street and hoping to get big money from Big Agriculture, the very entities profiting off the labor of foreign workers without working papers.

In preparation for the Ag Summit, Bob and I took a two-hour drive to Denison, a small town in western Iowa. Located in Crawford County, it is chock-full of hog and cattle slaughterhouses and meatpacking plants. The sign on the town water tower reads "It's a Wonderful Life," an homage to Donna Reed, a local farm girl who made good and starred in the famous Hollywood picture of the same name opposite Jimmy Stewart.

Present-day Denison looked nothing like small-town Bedford Falls. Parked outside the Tyson beef plant at shift change, Bob and I filmed the workers on their way home. To the naked eye, there was not one white or black person filing out of the factory. It was a sea of Latinos. According to the U.S. Census, Denison's population was nearly half Hispanic, an overwhelming number having migrated from Mexico. This was no accident. Back in the mid-'80s there were virtually no Hispanics living in Denison. The packing plants were unionized and paying more than $10 an hour, with benefits. Across the country, Americans made a livelihood working in the meat plants, bought a house, raised children, sent them to college, and retired. Americans worked these jobs. And the companies made money. But competition within the industry, a push for higher profits, and calamitous union strikes in Denison and across the United States led to steep wage and benefit cuts. Then the Latinos began arriving.

I've worked in slaughterhouses in both Alaska and North Carolina. The jobs are grueling, low-wage, and mostly filled by Mexicans. The average hourly wage, adjusted for inflation, had fallen in the nation's meatpacking plants by 50 percent over the last three decades, according to both government and industry statistics. In the meantime, the retail price of meats—again adjusted for inflation—had gone through the roof. The price for a pound of bacon over those same thirty years, for instance, had risen by 60 percent.

Falling wages, rising prices. So what happened to all the money? It wasn't at the Los Primos laundromat located at the corner of Main Street in Denison or the Carlyle Memorials headstone company next to that. Had we become a nation of Louis the XVIs unwilling to prepare our own breakfast sausages? Or had we been priced out of the

American way of life by Third World labor and a push for profit by the Invisible Hand of Wall Street and their pets in Congress?

One thing was sure, the Third World man was living and working like a burro in Iowa, sending his dollars home where he would convert them into a fleet of taxicabs, or a convenience store, or a discotheque, preparing his retirement as a Second World man. The Invisible Hand had created more middle-class Mexicans than Mexico ever had. And in that time, the Mexicans had become the biggest influx of foreign-born workers in the history of the United States.

The First World man, on the other hand, the one born in Iowa, would lose ground, worry about his home and his retirement because the only export from his small town was his children to the Big City. He would retire a Second World man. That might be encouraging mathematics for the CEOs and the Think Tanks in their employ. But to the First World man, the proposition was a calamity.

As the Agricultural Summit media confabulation was being convened, some of the country's largest meat producers, including Tyson, were announcing record earnings. Somewhere in those balance sheets lay the answer to declining wealth and earning power in rural America.

In Iowa there are six hogs to every human. And most of the humans are white, Christian, and attached to farming in some form or another. But look past the stereotypes and you see a streak of libertarianism here, a live-and-let-live manner of conducting oneself. Iowa voted for Barack Obama twice in the presidential elections. It was the third state in the Union to sanction gay marriage. And then again, despite its people's work ethic, Iowa was the top recipient of government welfare to farmers. Tens of billions of dollars of free money to prop up farming poured in every year from Washington, most of which went *not* to Ma and Pa Kettle, but to the wealthiest agricultural oligarchs. For example, the summit's host, Bruce Ras-tetter, had grown so rich from federal ethanol subsidies for gasoline additives that he was able to summon most of the Republican hope-fuls to come to the frozen ground of Iowa to kiss his boots. He was also a hog baron, and there was no telling how many, if any, illegal immigrants were employed at his factory farms.

The summit was packed with Iowans in tracksuits and overalls and plaid shirts. They were kept away from the candidates by cor-dons and wooden barricades. The protesters—Chicken Man, Cow Boy, Growth Hormone Girl, and more—were kept outside altogether and across the street from the pavilion. The press too were forbid-den to approach, roped off as the candidates strutted to the stage along a rubber carpet. As a member of the press, one could dutifully watch the officially sanctioned "conversation" between Rastetter and the White House hopefuls from a large video screen, and after-ward, if the candidate was desperate or dull enough, he would come to the "spin room" to speak with the press, the room being nothing more than an attached wedding tent just off the toilets—staffed with Latinos.

*¡Es una vida maravillosa, mi amigo!* It's a wonderful life, my friend.

*¡Sí, sí! Muy cierto, mi amigo.* How true, my friend.

There was old Lindsey Graham, the senior senator from South Carolina, standing around the snack table laden with ham sand-wiches waiting to be noticed. Good old Lindsey. A true 1 percenter—I'm talking 1 percent in the polls here, not in the pocketbook. Good old Senator Graham, growing stiff along with the bran muffins.

Hey, there's Mike Huckabee, former governor of Arkansas. Huck's drawing a crowd after delivering the best zinger of the day when Hog Baron Bruce asked him about undocumented agricul-tural workers.

The question is, Huckabee told the crowd, what do we do to stem the tide of people rushing over because they have heard that there's a bowl of food just across the border?

It got big applause, what they call red meat for the base, but it was more hypocrisy all the same. Tyson Foods is based in Arkansas. John Tyson was a big contributor to Huckabee. Tyson and Huckabee are great pals. Huckabee granted in-state tuition in Arkansas for the children of undocumented immigrants. This guy was a walking contradiction. I wormed my way close: Hey Gov, you been to Denison? If we run all the illegals out of Iowa, who's gonna butcher the bacon?

Huck half dodged the question with an answer about securing the border first and then worrying about the illegals after that, which said nothing about the workers and deteriorating wages today. Perfect politico response. Blame it on Washington. Refer the problem to Washington. Wait thirty years for nothing to happen in Washington. Wash. Rinse. Repeat. In the background, Huckabee's sour-faced handler was silently motioning for security to have me hauled out of there. She looked like a spawning salmon as her lips pantomimed the words: *Get him out.*

No problem, lady, I got what I needed, which was a whole lot of gas, nothing, emptiness. I'll show myself out. As Bob and I stepped away from the surging scrum, another camera filled our space.

The scene was what is known in the business as Bad TV. No access. Empty sound bites. Blue power suits. This would never do for our local viewership across the country. You want empty political-speak, you tuned in to nightly network news or cable TV.

We had to do something, and quick. A friend from a national political magazine pointed out to us that the candidates were arriving by the side door in the so-called "secure area," where police and Secret Service types were keeping the presidential hopefuls safe and away from Chicken Man. The satellite trucks were also parked in the secure zone, broadcasting the obtuse event live to the world. I was quite sure not a solitary soul in the world was watching.

Bob and I walked around to the gate of the secure zone and I told the state trooper manning the entrance that I needed to speak with the engineer in the satellite truck.

ID please.

NEWS MEDIA PRESS OFFICIAL IDENTIFICATION.

The trooper waved us through.

Not being one to misrepresent myself, I knocked on the door of the truck, introduced myself to the befuddled engineer, shook his hand, asked about his children. Good. Good. Very well then, nice to meet you. Then we stood off to the side and waited for their Lordships to arrive.

First it was Jeb! Please call him Jeb. I put my arm around Jeb, he slid his around my waist. Real pals now, me and Jeb. You in the race, Jeb? My mom wants to know.

Really?

Well . . . no . . . not really. She thinks you're the lying establishment a-hole. And don't you believe your pals in the smoke-filled backroom, Jeb. You don't have a shot. That pathway to amnesty thing for illegals? Brave. Humane. But it's not going to fly, Jeb. Besides, you're taking big money from Tyson too. That's okay. So is Hillary. Good flight home, Jeb. Say hey to your brother.

And hey, where *is* Hillary, Governor Rick Perry? She was invited by Hog Baron Bruce too. You think she's shredding email this afternoon? Nothing? You gotta go? Good luck with that grand jury indictment, sir.

Governor George Pataki. Swell guy. Yes, let's hug it out. New York in the house. I may have voted for you before. I'm not sure. Anyway, sir, you say leave the question of same-sex marriage to the states. But isn't it all same sex after you've been married long enough? Not for you, maybe? Ha! Haa! Good one, sir.

Shit, Governor P, here comes Ted. I'd run. He's wishing you good luck. Break a leg, he says? Don't trust him, Gov. He wants you to break a leg, then you just may have to sign up for Obamacare. Imagine the headlines: *Pataki Campaign Limps Along*. No sir, avoid him.

Of course, Senator Ted, you *may* just add one little thing to the last ten minutes of nothing you said before. Mmm-hmmm. Yes. Yes. I see . . . Hey, Ted, give me back my microphone.

There's Scott Walker over there. The front-runner. The union buster. Governor Walker. Governor, sir! A moment. Can you clarify your position on evolution, sir? Is Darwinism a left-wing conspiracy, sir? No comment. Sir? Your flip-flop on ethanol welfare. You're for it now? Or against it still? Sir, I'm noticing those are Wisconsin plates on your vehicles. Are you using Wisconsin government property to interview for a new job? If so, how is that fiscally responsible . . . sir?

Walker slipped away without a word. Weasel. I knew then his campaign was doomed.

It was obvious something was missing among the Republicans. They were not ready for prime time. Unless this was prime time. If it was, then we were in worse trouble than I'd thought. When the dude in a chicken suit squawking out front is making more sense than the dozen front-runners, you know something was missing. What the Republicans needed was someone with pizzazz, someone possessing some sizzle. Collectively, this field was a subprime slab of meat: Vienna weenies, flank steak, chuck filet. Pick your metaphor.

What this show required—and would soon get—was some red meat royalty, a Sir Loin of Beef wrapped in bacon and dipped in Marla Maples.

*The cities were coming unglued while the political leadership dandied about in Brylcream and man girdles, eating barbecue and gladhanding in swing states like Iowa. The American urban core might as well have been on another continent, for all the presidential candidates were talking about it.*

*Yet reports of police brutality on unarmed young black men continued to fill the airwaves. It was starting to make me wonder: Was this a predictable moment in the violent and absurd cycle that repeats itself every fifty years or so in American life? Or was this an exaggerated discontent fueled by the continuous loop of heinous ten-second clips recycled over and over on cable news?*

*One thing for sure, the summer of 2015 would be a long and violent one, but nothing like the hot, bloody summer of 1968.*

*Then, more than a hundred cities burned in the wake of the assassination of Dr. Martin Luther King Jr. at the hands of James Earl Ray, a white supremacist. Among the worst of the riots were in Baltimore and Chicago.*

*Murder was on the rise, but so was it too in 1968. Chicago set a record then, surpassing six hundred homicides for the first time in its history.*

*On the political front, Senator Robert F. Kennedy was assassinated by Sirhan Sirhan, an Arab nationalist, after winning the California Democratic primary.*

*The Democratic National Convention was held in Chicago and ended in a riot between police and antiwar protesters. George Wallace, the segregationist governor of Alabama, won forty-six electoral votes. In the end, the country elected Richard Milhous Nixon, and you know how that worked out.*

*At the same time, the membership of the Black Panther Party was awaiting trial for separate incidents of ambushing and assassinating California police officers. The Weathermen, a homegrown leftist terrorist group that would embark on a campaign of domestic bombings, was convening its first meetings in Ann Arbor, Michigan. College campuses across the nation were being seized by student protesters. Riots broke out at Columbia University in New York.*

*The existential threat of ISIS? Forget about it. The bloodiest week of the Vietnam War for American servicemen came in February 1968 as the Vietcong launched the Tet offensive.*

*Then consider that fifty years earlier, in the summer of 1919, more than three dozen cities burned in the great race riots that consumed the nation. Again, it happened in Baltimore and most spectacularly in Chicago. Over the course of a week during what came to be known as the Red Summer, thirty-eight people—twenty-three blacks and fifteen whites—were killed in Chicago and the homes of a thousand families burned at the hands of both black and white mobs. People were pulled from trolley cars and summarily executed. Violence was quelled in the Windy City only after the state militia was called out.*

*In the aftermath, the city assembled an integrated Commission on Race Relations to study the causes of the riot. Its findings,* The Negro in Chicago: A Study of Race Relations and a Race Riot, *were published in 1922, but could have just as easily been published today.*

*"The traditional ostracism, exploitation and petty daily insults to which they are continually exposed have doubtless provoked, even*

in normal-minded Negroes, a pathological attitude toward society," the report read in part.

"A desire for social revenge might well be expected to result from the facetious and insulting manner in which Negroes are often treated by officers of the law."

The current time in American cities was tumultuous, no doubt. People were angry, the resentment amplified by social media where crowds could be called to action in a matter of minutes. People were now armed to the teeth, having legally stockpiled military-grade weaponry. Mass shooters slaughtering innocents was almost a monthly happening now. That much was different.

But where were we, really, as a society? The end of days? Or treading somewhere just below sea level?

One thing was certain. TV wasn't offering much perspective. We were busy yodeling out our assholes, a twenty-four-hour chorus of the Sky Is Falling.

# Silver Bullet

BALTIMORE (SPRING)—

Freddie Gray Jr. was carrying a switchblade. That's the reason the Baltimore cops gave for arresting him. Then the cops took him for a ride. By the time the ride was over, Freddie, a thin, underweight black man, was in a coma.

A week later, Freddie died from the spinal cord injuries he somehow sustained from his journey. Violence erupted in the black quarter of town, which comprised two-thirds of the town. A group of agitators attacked fans going to the Orioles game, and the fans had to remain cowering inside the stadium throughout the evening. Police beat a press photographer. Shards of glass. Puffs of smoke. The cops, not wishing a Ferguson, stood down. Baltimore mayor Stephanie Rawlings-Blake later said that most of the protesters were peaceful, *although we also gave those who wished to destroy space to do that as well.*

Say what?

Where were the leaders?

After Freddie's funeral, Baltimore burned in earnest: twelve dozen vehicles, five dozen buildings, twenty-four dozen drug stores looted, and twenty dozen arrests. The crowd shelled a TV news crew with bottles. For days the streets were a pyre of discontent and shattered glass.

Standing not a mile from the epicenter of the recent unrest, it was easy to see why. The row housing was boarded up and falling down. Schools were underfunded, overcrowded, substandard, and peeling despite the fact that casino gambling had been approved by voters to increase financing for education. The previous mayor had been convicted of stealing gift cards intended for the poor. The few green spaces were littered with bottles and paper scraps and surly-looking adults. Quarantined along Greenmount Avenue, young black men walked idly around, apparently with nothing to do. Unemployment for their demographic hovered around 40 percent.

A lack of money has got as much to do with the state of urban unrest as rogue cops. At least that's what a young black dope slinger on a Baltimore corner told me, confirming the nexus of race and class that I had been seeing and hearing across the country.

The trailer park probably feels it, he said, answering my question. But the ghetto feels it first.

That's when we heard the cop bark: I thought I told you motherfuckers to clear off the corner!

There were three of them. Meaty white men in uniform and Kevlar vests but no caps. Their belligerence was startling considering the city was a tinderbox of black versus blue. Nevertheless, the dope man turtled up into a meek round-shouldered passivity. The police here had a long, outrageous history of misconduct. In the past four years, according to the *Baltimore Sun,* the city had paid out $5.7 million to settle more than a hundred police brutality claims.

Dope man knew it. Gauging by his reaction, the dope man may have been taken for a ride at some point or another, himself.

The officer made it clear that he wasn't just talking to the black men, he was also talking to me and the cameramen. From his point of view, it seemed, the racial arithmetic here was simple.

White guy + Black guy = Dope deal

I pointed to our cameras. I offered the officers my press card. I fumbled my way through a nonchalant cigarette and a defense of the First Amendment before finally fucking off. The guy scared me. His perspiration, girth, intensity all unnerved me. This was *his* corner.

Kentucky senator Rand Paul was on the high-speed silver train the night Charm City burned, traveling from Wall Street to Washington, D.C. He had announced his bid for the Republican nomination for president a few weeks earlier, claiming he was the one white man who understood and could cure the ills of the black ghetto. His social analysis of the plague that infected black Baltimore: a lack of fathers.

Speaking on a conservative radio talk show the day following the riot, our fainthearted senator confessed: I came through Baltimore on the train last night. I'm glad the train didn't stop.

I don't know what bothered me more: his unctuous "black fathers" drivel, or the fact that a guy asking us to elect him our leader was happy to avoid an American city desperately in need of a father figure, or the fact that he didn't know his train actually *had* stopped in Baltimore.

Not only did Paul not get off the train, but he apparently didn't even look out the window long enough to realize the train had pulled into Baltimore Penn Station. And somewhere in that lay the problem.

The train that the clueless senator rode makes its regular run between the twin towers of power: Wall Street and Washington. On the way, it logs short stops in crumbling cities of the Ghetto Belt—Newark, New Jersey; Philadelphia; Wilmington, Delaware. And, yes, Baltimore. But nobody with power ever seems to speak of or visit these places.

Consider that Manhattan has three of the five richest zip codes in America. The District of Columbia is also surrounded by a half dozen of the richest counties in the United States. In between are four of the poorest, most violent urban centers in the nation. It is a stretch of the country where the train has gone off the rails—even literally. Just a few weeks after Paul's journey, this very train would derail while coming into Philadelphia, killing eight and injuring two hundred more. Subsequent investigations would reveal that the reason for the accident was that the technology available to slow the train down was not in place, thanks in part to congressional dithering and woolgathering.

If one wished to know the direction and strength of the winds in America, it was better to read the weather vanes in these urban cores. It wasn't too long ago that American power lay in the industrial might of these cities, the largest in their respective states: shipping, steel, chemicals, automobiles. Washington minded the bureaucratic shop. Wall Street invested your savings relatively quietly. It was the cities in between that created the wealth of the nation.

So I took the train, disembarking at each stop to survey the New American Century.

A Latino mechanic in Newark told me that the issues went beyond race—that anybody in a position of power becomes, in effect, a

white man, whether it's a black cop or a Latino executive or the female president of the United States. Later, a bodega owner said he
wished that cops would spend more time in his violent neighborhood. More cops, less cops. What was the answer? I wondered.
Damned if you do, damned if you don't.

A white truck driver in Philadelphia said the next thing to blow
would be the white middle class, the people he believes are footing
the bill for everything and getting nothing in return, except a place
at the back of the line. The Philadelphia school district was broke
and downsizing. Children could not take books home and yet tens
of thousands of books were moldering in a warehouse, scattered all
over the floor, the boxes unsealed and broken. Embarrassed authorities would not let our camera, or any TV camera, in to see them.
We managed to get in through a disgruntled union official anyway.

A part-time plumber in Wilmington made a grand sweep with
his hand as he said that he, like so many other Americans, would
need to work until the day he dies. All but gone are the good jobs
that used to be here at Chrysler and DuPont.

The plumber was standing in front of 1209 North Orange Street,
an unremarkable, single-level building with a pea-green awning.
The views from its windows included run-down row housing and
a parking garage. Inside 1209 was another matter. Operated by
CT Corporation, the building was the legal address of more than
250,000 businesses ranging from Wall Street banks to industrial
giants like General Electric and Boeing, firms that often managed
to pay nothing in federal income taxes. Delaware, like the Cayman
Islands, is a tax haven, its laws designed to help multinational companies avoid shelling out for common-good projects like schools
and roads. Even LLCs linked to Hillary Clinton and Donald Trump
had drop boxes inside.

After my time with the dope man in Baltimore, I waited at

Baltimore's Penn Station for the next train out of town, thinking of America's great racial Berlin Walls: 60th Street in Chicago, Delmar Boulevard in St. Louis, 8 Mile Road in Detroit, Greenmount Avenue in Baltimore. And who should walk in but former secretary of state James Baker III, alone, by himself, without security. The only politician I had seen in the city, unscripted, without expectation of a camera. I introduced myself and he seemed surprised that anyone should know who he was. The greatest diplomat of twentieth-century America, I told him. Why should I not know? Iraq. Russia. Palestine. I asked him his opinion on Baltimore. He put it as simply as the dope man.

So much wealth in the black communities has been lost, he said. We've got to find a way to get some money, some jobs to these people, or I'm afraid we haven't seen our last fire.

*Why is there so much violence but so little else on local TV news?*

*Because murder is easy. Shootings are sometimes amusing and a TV reporter can turn such filler around in a matter of minutes. The self-contained simplicity of mayhem makes it a highly profitable television enterprise.*

*Take the true-life example of two knucklehead police detectives nicknamed Pooky and Willy. It's a warm summer evening. Children are out. Frothy drinks are being had. Pooky is hanging with his crew on one side of the street in front of an abandoned school. Willy is partying with his boys on a porch on the other side of the street.*

*A cross-boulevard argument breaks out between Pooky and Willy over who makes the best Kool-Aid.*

*How best to make Kool-Aid? Sugar and water. There is no other way to make Kool-Aid, excepting for the odd dash of lime. But that is beside the point. The point is the disrespect one man utters about another man's culinary skills. Guns are pulled, shots are fired, two innocent bystanders—children—are ferried to the hospital.*

*TV combs the scene now. People on the block give interviews.*

*What's this world coming to? says one.*

*He had so much life in front of him, says another.*

*And so forth.*

*If a reporter is particularly lucky, he may elicit a tear or two.*

*There is crime tape and an official police report. This nutshell of the human drama can be cranked out in forty minutes. It can take* even less time depending on the reporter's skill or a request for a live shot from the director's desk. It's like making melted-cheese sandwiches. You can flip them all day long.

We reporters rarely ask questions about that abandoned school: why it still stands or why children don't learn. Or why police detectives have not managed to apprehend either Pooky or Willy, much less ascertained their real names. Or why handguns are as easy to come by as Tic Tacs. Questions like these muck things up. Slow the process. Mess up the money.

We will not admit it in the course of our Emmy acceptance speeches, but we reporters know that our work has a corrosive effect, amplifying anxiety in the suburban kitchen. It reinforces stereotypes of a violent black city, which may have its truths, but the extent of the violence is blown wildly out of proportion.

Watching TV, you'd think the whole city was bleeding cherry red.

# Red Summer in White City

The problem with Chicago is geography.

It is a giant, sprawling, segregated city where men cannot cross forbidden streets, alleyways, or expressways. To do so is to gamble recklessly with one's life.

Yet still, men gamble. After trending downward for some years, murder and gunplay in the city were back in fashion. There had been more than two hundred killings so far in Chicago—a 15 percent increase and summer had not yet officially begun. Good thing they can't shoot straight in the Windy City, one cop told me, because there had also been more than a thousand nonfatal shootings. We get one gun off the street, two more come, he said.

One astute statistician calculated that more Americans had been murdered in Chicago in the last fifteen years than had died in Iraq and Afghanistan combined. Much of the mayhem was happening on the South and West sides. The black and brown sides. What they were now calling with metaphorical flair Chi-Raq, thanks to the work of that number-cruncher.

Police in America knocking black heads, racially profiling, turning out pockets, manipulating evidence, killing under the flimsiest of circumstances. Big historic problems magnified by the technological innovations of cell phones and live streaming and social media that can put any situation out to the world in seconds along with directions and a Google map to the unrest.

But there was also the other side of things: A black person in the United States is six times more likely as a proportion of his population to be the victim of a murder than a white person, and eight times more likely to be the murderer. Black-on-black violence results in a huge police presence. The police presence results in the stuff of headlines. Black-on-black crime received little analysis I noticed, no mention beyond the "bleeds it ledes" offerings of local TV news.

Chicago too was going off the rails. The smoke from the urban core was thick this season. Something substantial, interconnected was happening. As much as we were tired of death and disorder, we made the drive from Detroit, a city with a murder rate more than twice that of Chicago.

Whenever I travel, I avoid the corridors of power, the clubs of high importance, the restaurants with starched tablecloths. You'll get no answers to real life there. You have to go to the alley. And so a meeting with a group of men was arranged on a South Side back street by Jedidiah Brown, a young, energetic bordering on high-strung black man doing triple duty as a minister, social worker, and candidate for city council.

Brown made it his business to be at every shooting on the South Side, thinking his mediating presence might somehow improve things. His telephone, it was easy to see, was radioactive, a repository of contacts for cops and robbers, priests and dope pushers. The chief of police himself was one call away.

In fact, the cops called him as we were driving around, taking a look at the landscape of the rugged West Side. They were giving him directions to a shooting on the South Side. The reporter in me marveled at his access. The cops calling like a Chinese restaurant calling to tell him his Szechuan beef was ready for pickup.

I am not the best gauger of destitution, my judgment having been warped by years of reporting in Detroit. By comparison, in cities like St. Louis and Chicago and Los Angeles, the "ghettos" appear relatively nice. Livable. No falling-in porches. In West Side Chicago, the streets were paved and swept. The apartment buildings occupied. The grass cut and the stores full. What was more, there was foot traffic. Women walking freely about their business, shopping bags hanging from their forearms. A child riding a tricycle. How normal. How tranquil. A beguiling mirage of American middle-class life.

As we turned left off the boulevard onto a wide side street, the leftovers of a crime scene unfolded. A yellow caution ribbon, squad cars, an elderly man hanging out his window. Somebody had been shot in the vestibule of the apartment building. This was our proverbial Chinese restaurant. Brown, by virtue of his telephone, slipped under the police tape, spoke with detectives, slipped back out from the shooting scene, and made a direct line to the dope boys on the corner. He'd make a great reporter, I thought.

Nobody seen nothing, said one teenager.

That's how it goes, homey, said another.

Getting few answers, and no converts to his unsolicited offers of mediation, an exasperated Brown climbed back in his sedan and drove us toward the beleaguered Woodlawn neighborhood where we were to meet some men. He took the southbound Dan Ryan Expressway. Shoot-to-thrill riflemen were having their fun this

season, the count so far being nine random shootings on city free-
ways in twenty-two days, some during rush hour.

On we drove. Once known as White City and the "city of a million electric lights" for the magnificent amusement park there with
plaster-of-Paris buildings, the Woodlawn community like so many
other South Side neighborhoods was awash in darkness and
violence.

I'm down with the struggle, Brown said as we pulled onto a
street that was indeed boarded up and had mammoth speed bumps
designed to slow down dope deals and drive-bys. But the struggle
has so many branches, he continued. The politicians, the churches,
the streets themselves. It's really difficult sometimes to keep your
focus on the trees. There's just a vacuum of leadership. Honestly,
nobody seems to care unless it's in the news.

On a street not far from a playground, we pulled up to a group of
older men. They were not the young street employee entrepreneur
types, but the next rung up. Lieutenants, not soldiers. Like Brown,
they exuded a calm, cold desperation, hoods and ball caps covering
their heads.

I got to give you credit, one of the men said, noticing Bob's pasty
calves beckoning from his camo shorts. You got some balls coming here.

Why are black men slaughtering each other? I nakedly asked
one of the men who was dressed in a dark hoodie and sweatpants.
He was handsome, goateed, and worn. Not old, but not young. Sul-
len and intense. He gave me no name. So I called him Dude.

We're bust in our communities, Dude said. We're overpopu-
lated. Look around. Do you see any stores? Do you see any places
where anybody can work? It's not enough jobs for a third of us . . .
any of us. We're standing in front of an abandoned building.

We in fact were standing in front of an empty brick building.

But it was well kept in its way. It did not appear as though it had been stripped of its copper wiring or hot-water tank. It didn't look like junkies used it as a shooting gallery. It wasn't pissed on with graffiti. There was a park across the street. Children played. The grass of the adjacent building was mowed. No, this was "nice." Nothing compared to Detroit.

Dude, who described his occupation as a minder of his own business, was an informed man. Consider: Black unemployment tops 25 percent in Chicago, as compared to 7 percent for whites and 12 percent for Latinos. That number skyrockets to 92 percent for black teenagers.

Another man, this one much larger than Dude, said a man's gonna do.

Do what? I didn't have to ask. I knew the answer, but I did just the same.

A man is going to do whatever he thinks he's got to do to eat. And if he has to eat another man or another man's children to feed himself, then *bon appétit*, motherfucker. I stood there thinking of the good ol' boy I'd met in Alabama. The one with the freezer full of squirrel. A man's gonna eat. Same with Ciro, wearing flip-flops in the reeds of the Rio Grande. *¡Buen provecho, cabrón!*

A third member of the crew, a man with a tattooed neck who was dressed in a Captain America T-shirt, explained the attractiveness of warring with your own. Black men couldn't fight city hall. They couldn't fight police. They couldn't fight globalization. But they could battle the shadow across the alley. They could fight him for control of low-slung buildings with their windows smashed out. They could fight him for title to the local playground. They could war for the drug business of black and white customers alike. The arithmetic is basic: You do him before he does you.

Some people gotta die, said Captain America.

Some of the men had done time. Two-thirds of the inmates at Chicago's Cook County Jail were black and doing a bid for drug sales or drug possession, according to Sheriff Tom Dart. The intake cells there smelled like horse paddocks. It was a dank and gray facility with no natural light penetrating the walls. The jail is the largest in the United States and so overcrowded that it has been under federal oversight since 1980. It is also the largest mental health hospital in the country, where one in three inmates suffers some sort of mental disorder. Men incarcerated along with their demons make the Cook County jailhouse a very dangerous place.

Jails are for violent people, and we have a lot of those, Dart said. But what about the nonviolent people, the mentally ill? They don't need to be here. And honestly, I don't know why they are.

The branch of government with which black Chicagoans most frequently dealt seemed to be the criminal justice system. Police who drove through South Side neighborhoods were routinely greeted by teenagers with a wave of the middle finger.

Recently there had been well-chronicled reports of abuse in the Chicago Police Department: a commander sticking his firearm into the mouth of a suspect, police dropping teenagers into rival gang territories, and so on. Adding to the dissonance were the denials of Chicago's superintendent of police, Garry McCarthy. When asked about the ongoing violence, McCarthy got snippy.

There are a lot less shootings than there were last year, he said. I don't know if you are aware of that?

I wasn't aware of that, because according to numbers supplied by McCarthy's own Chicago Police Department, shootings were up 20 percent. Spouting dumb shit like that in the midst of a crime wave can cost a man his job. And eventually it did. McCarthy was fired a few months later, with murder spiraling out of control and the emergence of a videotape that the city had tried to suppress showing a police officer shooting unarmed teenager Laquan McDonald sixteen times, killing him.

McDonald was a ward of the state, a dropout who enrolled himself in an alternative high school in an attempt to get his life together. But Chicago's schools, already underperforming and underfunded, especially in black sections of the city, weren't the places to get your life together. Mayor Rahm Emanuel had closed nearly fifty public schools, many on the South Side. Now the school buildings sat empty, mocking, while the students went off to other classrooms that were already overcrowded. One elementary had a kindergarten class with fifty-one children and a first-grade class with forty-eight.

More outrageous, the superintendent of schools had recently resigned under a federal corruption probe, having allegedly steered $20 million in no-bid contracts to her own company. Stealing from the future of her own students.

And then there were the sweeteners siphoned off for the politically connected. A hotel chain received $55 million of the city's property tax money to help subsidize a skyscraper it was building downtown. One of Mayor Emanuel's contributors owns a hedge fund that is part owner of that hotel chain.

Hizzoner was no stranger to high finance. In fact, he was brilliant at it. Consider that in between stints at the Clinton White House and the U.S. House of Representatives, Emanuel worked as an investment banker. In just thirty months, he reportedly raked in $18 million in compensation despite the fact that he had absolutely no experience in finance. So no doubt, Rahm—who also served as Obama's chief of staff before being elected the mayor of Chicago—knew money, or at least knew where to find it.

And property tax money, it is worth remembering, goes to pay for public schools. And, again, the schools on the South Side were being shuttered as in Baltimore and Detroit and Philly. The business community and the mayor argued that the skyscraper would bring jobs. Maybe. But that's not how they were seeing it from the South Side.

The mayor's people promised us an interview at a hotel where he was giving a speech. After the speech, the mayor decided to drive away. One of his security people stumbled over the curb trying to keep us at bay. I was getting the picture. Downtown Chicago was doing great. Public money pumped into private development projects. But few jobs went to South Siders.

This was by no means the Chicago of 1919. The city was not in flames. The beaches were integrated. Roaming bands of white marauders were not pulling people off of streetcars and murdering them. Blacks were not sniping at white motorists driving through the neighborhoods. (The rash of freeway shootings notwithstanding.) People's homes certainly were not on fire. Imagine today what that would look like through the amplifiers of TV and social media.

Chicago was not on fire, but fumes were steaming from the neighborhood streets. Blacks originally made the great migration north to Chicago for the work and the better material life that factory jobs brought. But today, the manufacturing jobs were scarce, and one of the few careers left is holding down the corner. Nabisco announced it was eliminating half the jobs at its biggest Chicago-based plant and spending millions of dollars to upgrade its Mexican facility. Good for business. Bad for the neighborhood. A never-ending swirl toward the drain.

Guns are a problem, and they flood in illegally from nearby Indiana. The courts and prosecutors are a problem, cutting back on weapons cases because the jails are so full. But the real color problem is green, one of the men on the corner said, echoing men on the corner everywhere. People around here don't got it. Then you're fighting like rats.

And so the corner must be defended.

Can't you just get away? I asked Dude. I may as well have been asking if he had the power of resurrection.

By what method? he hissed. By what means?

The rain started falling like marbles. The men began to scatter.

Remember us, one said, pulling up his hood. Somebody ain't gonna be here in the future. Death, son. That's the way it goes.

That man was a prophet.

Because the following week, one of the crew who went by the name Chubb stepped out on the wrong side of town. Chubb caught a bullet and then Chubb caught a ride in an ambulance. His buddy was not so lucky. He caught a ride to the morgue.

Presidents of the United States are not best known for their hairstyles: Dwight Eisenhower had not a forehead, but a five-head. John Adams? An abomination resembling a boiled egg. Lyndon B. Johnson and Richard M. Nixon sported the same swept-back widow's peak, frustrating American men's fashion for an entire decade. The most famous of presidential follicular adornment most certainly belonged to George Washington, who paraded about in a powdered mullet curled on the edges. Historians now inform us that this was in fact the general's real hair.

Monstrosities all, no doubt. But the lowly comb-over—reeking of insincerity and something to hide—has been a White House rarity. If the paintings from the National Portrait Gallery are to be taken at face value, then the only president to have sported a true comb-over was William Henry Harrison. Sweeping from back to front and serving only to highlight an already ample and unattractive nose, the coif did nothing to keep the ninth president of the United States warm. Refusing to wear an overcoat during his inaugural address in January 1841, Harrison contracted pneumonia and died in office a month later. He was, ironically, a member of the Whig Party.

And now came this . . .

# Don à l'Orange

We were back from the alleys of Chicago, rolling through videotape in our office while trying to chip golf balls into a Styrofoam cup we'd taped to a filing cabinet. The television set was on. There was a black spot on the screen marking where it had been struck by an errant shot. Donald Trump was holding a press conference. He was announcing a run for president. The electronic bruise made it look as though Trump had been socked in the forehead with an iron skillet.

How many times is this guy gonna pull the chain? I said to Bob, lining up a ball.

Ever the master showman, Trump seemed to yank the presidential chain every election cycle. He toyed with it back in '88 while hawking his book *The Art of the Deal*. He never actually entered the race then, but the publicity helped make the book a number one best seller.

Trump actually sort of got into the 2000 contest at the behest of Jesse Ventura, the former professional wrestler turned governor of Minnesota, and Roger Stone, the former Nixon dirty trickster and ultimate Beltway insider. He pulled fifteen thousand votes in the California primary as a Reform Party candidate before bowing out to the knuckle-dragging conservative Pat Buchanan, whom he referred to unmercilessly as a "Hitler lover." He threatened to run again in 2004, this time very seriously, very seriously, he said. And why not? He was shopping a reality TV show. In 2008, he told the *New York Post* he was thinking about it, until he forgot about it. He teased us again during the 2012 cycle, with polls showing he was the leading potential Republican candidate. He repeatedly barked for President Obama's birth certificate, until, you know, he decided he wasn't running anymore.

Now he was back, really prepared to do it, maybe.

No one seemed to have told him that this was supposed to be Jeb versus Hillary, the epic confrontation between members of the imperial families of American politics. The power brokers and the money class had all but decided that they were the nominees, the cash and the endorsements all sewn up. But here comes Don, the preposterous, pompous, outrageous New York developer. Here comes the sizzle.

Trump appeared heavy, having packed on some noticeable pounds, his tailored jacket hanging on him like a wrinkled maternity robe. His skin was an unnatural hue of orange. And his hair. Was that a comb-over? Was it a weave? What color was it exactly? On my TV screen, he looked like a gigantic piece of candy corn with the orange top and the bruised face.

But Trump did not disappoint. He was bombastic and bilious: "The other candidates," he said of his soon-to-be-GOP rivals, "they went in, they didn't know the air-conditioning didn't work. They sweated like dogs. They didn't know the room was too big because they didn't have anybody there."

That's true, I said to Bob, reminding him of the Iowa clown show.

". . . I'm using my own money. I'm not using the lobbyists'. I'm not using donors. I don't care. I'm really rich . . ."

Trump was blistering the political hacks, claiming they had turned First World workers into secondhand discount shoppers:

". . . How stupid are our leaders? How stupid are these politicians who allow this to happen? How stupid are they?"

Yep. That was a good one too. It was going to play. Trump had by now worked himself up into a plump berry of bombast:

". . . I will be the greatest jobs president that God ever created!"

He was funny. These were going to be good ratings. Terrific ratings. These were going to be the best ratings you've ever seen. Believe me.

Then Trump turned bigot: "When Mexico sends its people, they're not sending their best. They're not sending you . . . They're sending people that have lots of problems and they're bringing those problems [to] us. They're bringing drugs, they're bringing crime, they're rapists, and some, I assume, are good people."

Rapists? Well, that puts a fork in it, Bob said, turning away. He's done.

One would have assumed. Trump thought Mexicans were rapists. Trump was going to build a wall to keep them out. It was already being looped on the ticker at the bottom of the screen. "Trump: Mexicans Are Rapists."

The Don was done five minutes after he'd begun. A world record flameout.

But then Trump also said something you wouldn't expect from a billionaire with a butler who lives in his own office tower high over midtown Manhattan: "Sadly, the American dream is dead. But if I get elected president I will bring it back bigger and better and stronger than ever before, and we will make America great again."

*Make America great again.* He nailed it, I thought. He must have workshopped it, had it polled, overheard it from the hard hats on one of his construction jobs. The establishment right was still peddling the outdated notion of American transcendence. We were the greatest, strongest, most virile nation on the planet. Romney tried that line in 2012, but didn't really believe it. After all, he had secretly denounced nearly half the American population as deadbeats suckling on the government teat. But in defense of Slick Mitt, who *did* believe it anymore? We had lost our wealth, our work, our way. The cities were destitute and on fire. The infrastructure was crumbling. The famous Chicago Skyway toll road had become as rough as a cheese grater and was sold to a foreign company for $2 billion to plug a short-term budget hole. Chi-Town's parking meters went for an additional $1 billion. Pensions and health care had been slashed in Detroit to make room for the largest municipal bankruptcy in American history. Old women and crippled firefighters were given a couple hundred bucks a month, a pat on the head, and a "thanks for your service" before being tossed on the Obama health exchange. Former soldiers in Phoenix were dying while waiting for their appointments at the V.A. as administrators scurried to cover it up. And more servicemen and servicewomen were arriving home every day from our forever wars in the Middle East, wars that we had yet to pay for—preferring to burden our children rather than tax ourselves. What was *exceptional* about any of this?

At the same time the establishment left was bogged down in the narrative that America was never great, never exceptional, that it was racist and slothful. The way forward was more cosmopolitanism, greater globalism, open borders, and more generous benefits for the historically oppressed minority groups. Problems? Yes, the country had many, but there was little acknowledgment from the liberal elitist camp that ours was the most nimble, most rapidly changing culture in the world. It was a culture able to correct itself through law and reason. The archaeological ruins of the American Century lay everywhere, the empty machine shops and storefronts in both small towns and large, testaments to an economic greatness that was slipping away. Somehow Americans were racist and yet Obama earned 43 percent of the white vote in 2008 as the economy had collapsed under Republican control. Obama was offering hope and some change in our pockets. Americans of all colors thought they were voting for a new New Deal. What we got instead was health care and little else.

*Make America great again.* It was brilliant in its simplicity. It was the economy, stupid. It's always been the economy, stupid. And it was the fault of the government and the big banks. The Everyman had been forgotten and he was angry. We had seen this in our travels: low wages and strangled opportunities. It cut across all races. All parties. All regions. *Make it great again. Fix it. Help us.*

I turned to Matt and Bob.

We gotta track this guy down. He might be a clown, but he's on to something.

They agreed, but the Dawn of the Don would have to wait. The very next evening, a deranged white terrorist named Dylann Roof, precise and plotting in his hatred, murdered nine black parishioners as they worshipped in a South Carolina church. The man's hope was to ignite a race war.

# Knights in White Satin

The boss wanted us to head south. But I didn't want to go.

The media machine had pulled into Charleston, South Carolina, in the wake of the Emanuel AME Church massacre. Some good and meaningful stories had been filed, so the last thing I thought the town needed was one more Johnny-come-lately picking at the pain, shucking and conniving and manipulating some tears from a community that likely had none left to spare.

Well, how about the church burning, then? the boss asked.

Shortly after the Charleston horror, a historic black house of worship in rural South Carolina had gone up in flames. Arson was reported as the suspected cause. The Ku Klux Klan had burned the very same church to the ground twenty years before. What if they had done it again? Or some unaffiliated white supremacist like Roof? That made a compelling story line. The growing White Menace in the age of Trump and trigger-happy cops.

But it wasn't arson or the KKK that felled the church. It was a lightning strike. Natural circumstances. This fact had been reported, but nowhere near as widely and as breathlessly as the initial arson theory. And so the false fact of white terror stuck like soap residue. I had something else in mind.

The South Carolina legislature had been shamed into removing a Confederate flag from the statehouse grounds after a photograph surfaced of Roof posing with the old Dixie banner days before his murder rampage. The KKK was planning a rally on the capitol steps to protest its removal.

It was the stuff TV news was made of: a manufactured event, simple and self-contained. The recipe for this muffin consisted of a few sound bites from the rally, some flabby platitudes about brotherhood, the photo of Roof. Pop it all into the editing blender and you could produce something completely forgettable in a matter of hours. If there was violence, all the better. Violence meant clicks and retweets.

But again, I had something else in mind.

I called the KKK hotline—yes, the Klan had a hotline—and got a voice recording from the local Imperial Wizard, who, it would later be revealed, doubled as a snitch for the FBI: *We the Loyal White Knights of the Ku Klux Klan would like to say hail victory to the young warrior in South Carolina Dylann S. Roof, who decided to do what the Bible told him. An eye for an eye. A tooth for a tooth. They have spilled our blood too long. It's time we spilled theirs.*

The voice was heavy and menacing with a thick backwoods drawl. It made my flesh creep but I left my personal number anyway. Eventually, I got a call back.

The caller introduced himself as Will Quigg, the California Grand Dragon and West Coast King Kleagle of the Loyal White Knights of the Ku Klux Klan. He was, in short, the Head Honky in

Charge. Quigg informed me that he was flying in from Southern California to Greensboro, North Carolina, in a few days and would grant me and Matt permission to carpool with him to the rally.

I'm using you for propaganda, Quigg warned me.

I guess that makes us even, I said. I want to get a look at you up close.

The rendezvous was arranged.

Walking around the baggage claim around midnight, I noticed a thin, gristly man wearing sunglasses. He was dressed in a black shirt with a red cross on the left breast and short brown pants revealing pale, hairless legs. He didn't look like a Mormon missionary, so I took the chance.

You here for the Grand Dragon?

Yes sir, I am.

He gave his name as Calvin Simpson, a local Klansman who was there not only to provide some modicum of security for the Grand Dragon, but to make him look special, spruce him up with an entourage. How would it look for His Grandness to have to retrieve his own baggage?

Matt and I had spent the better part of a week in Simpson's neck of the woods, the rural counties north of Greensboro. If there was a hotbed of Klan extremism, then the area just off the fast-food and auto-parts strip malls along the Carolina-Virginia border was the place. The Loyal White Knights—one of the largest and most violent Klan factions in the United States—were headquartered in the small town of Eden, in a shabby trailer where no flag flew, Dixie or otherwise. The klavern, or local branch, maintained a post office box nearby. The Imperial Wizard made his home nearby. Klan picnics were held at his compound. Nationwide, this faction claimed about 150 members, but locally they kept such a low profile that the chapter president of the NAACP was surprised to learn they were based in his county.

Simpson and I made small talk in the terminal, where he revealed that he was unemployed and living off government food stamps.

A Klansman feeding from the public trough. Ironic.

I gotta pay for it, I complained.

Yeah, you got to pay for it, 'cause you're fortunate enough to have a full-time job.

He was a stereotype wrapped in an insignia, an unemployed white man who complained about deadbeat colored people sucking off the system, taking resources they weren't entitled to and multiplying. But in his eyes, his government handout had nothing to do with his lack of skill or work ethic. He was a victim of circumstances beyond his control, whether it was the brown horde from Mexico undercutting his hourly price for hanging sheetrock or the corporate cabal concocting a new world order that did not include him. It was a viewpoint common even among those members of the white working class who didn't spend their Saturday nights prancing around in satin robes and burning crosses. A subject to explore during the car ride, I thought.

As the Grand Dragon descended on the escalator, Simpson the lickspittle popped up like a cork bobber to greet him at the bottom with an obsequious arm-out palm-down salute. The men then hugged it out as a Muslim woman in a headscarf marveled at their public display of affection.

Quigg went to the counter and laid out his driver's license to rent a car. I pointed out to him that he was accepting help from a black man behind the counter—and informed the black man behind the counter that he was servicing a Klansman.

Simpson turned to me with annoyance: Why you trying to stir up problems?

Just pointing out the facts here.

We're Christians, sir, we try not to be rude.

Quigg's legal name was William Ernest Hagen. His address checked back to a tidy half-million-dollar powder-blue bungalow on a pleasant cul-de-sac in Orange, California, not five miles from Disneyland—the heart of multicultural America. A photograph of Hagen's home on Google Earth showed what appears to be a Latino gardener mowing the grass median the Grand Dragon shared with his neighbor. It truly is a small world after all.

Hagen, forty-nine, with a clipped mustache and short dark hair, bore a striking resemblance to Freddie Mercury, the showy, homosexual frontman of the '70s rock band Queen. I had expected him to be dressed in something more ostentatious, something more overt and "klanny" than the subdued khaki he was sporting now. Hagen explained that the robes were for ceremonial purposes only, normally white and satin, though "officers" were entitled to more vibrant hues of reds and purples. This subdued public garb he had on now, he said, gave members a more mainstream appearance, less intimidating to potential recruits and airline stewardesses.

The Grand Dragon found his car in the rental lot. A Chevy Spark, an eco-friendly subcompact, something a hipster might drive. I was expecting a Suburban, but penny wise, pound foolish, since the Grand Dragon gig was purely a ceremonial position that paid nothing.

Hagen arranged his luggage so as not to impair his line of sight. He took too much time arranging his rearview mirrors, and demanded complete silence as he inched nervously out onto the expressway like a bunny entering a strange garden. He immediately got lost in the labyrinth of concrete ribbon, turning east when he should have turned south, cussing and complaining about the GPS navigator with the Yankee accent.

Simpson sat in the back with me, still stewing about the scene at the rental car counter.

What were you doing? He was just an average guy doing his job.

But he was black. You don't deal with blacks, right?

We don't like it, but you got to mix with people. You can't hate all the time.

Excuse me? I thought that's what you do?

You got to deal with it, is all. That's how it is in America.

Again, there was something to be explored here, but Simpson's small light of revelation was smothered whole by Hagen, who dominated the trip with his poor driving and conversations and philosophies as dull as a butter knife. According to Hagen: Jesus was not a Jew, Catholics were not true Christians, and there was no Holocaust. Though when pressed on this last point, he relented a bit.

Okay, maybe a little Holocaust, but not as bad as they say.

Concerning Roof, the Grand Dragon said that despite the Imperial Wizard's telephone recording, the official Klan position on the subject was that it was wrong to kill black people while they worshipped. However, if a group of blacks had been dealing crack on a street corner, well, that was another matter altogether. As for mixed-raced people like myself? We would be the first to die in the great war, since we had no one to belong to, no place to go.

So here Matt and I were, careening down a dark rural highway, no one in the world knowing where we were. Me in the back holding a penlight to my face for the camera. Matt, crammed in the front passenger seat, filming, having gotten himself a raise of $1 an hour. The Klansmen could have turned off on any country road, taken us to the woods, and snuffed us. But these two were not masterminds of a master race. They didn't seem especially fit or hardened. They were dressed like package couriers wearing dark glasses at night, thinking it would prevent them from being recognizable on TV.

Frankly, I was more afraid of Hagen's driving. He lived near Los Angeles, he said, and these long, empty highways put him on edge. Already, he'd nearly put us into a cement barricade and Matt into the windshield. Furthermore, he continuously complained that it was hard to drive and conduct an interview at the same time.

I'd brought along a sleeve of saltine crackers for the trip, both as a snack and a prop. I leaned forward and offered one to Hagen.

Cracker?

He declined, not getting the joke.

Simpson did: Cracker? That's funny. Cracker. No shame in my game. None whatsoever.

He took two.

The saltines gave Simpson a dry mouth, and he suggested twice to Hagen that they stop and go halfsies on a two-liter of Coke. It took the Dragon two or three exits to muster the nerve to disembark, and when he did, he found himself at an ill-lighted gas station on the south side of town. The black side of town. The Spark bottomed out as he pulled into the station.

Simpson, dressed in his Klan duds, marched gamely into the store and bought the soda pop with cash. He was then refused use of the toilet by management. Black eyes followed his whiteness out the door and across the parking lot to the rental car. A local drunk was hitting up Hagen for change.

I guess they only let blacks use the toilet, Simpson said.

That's ironic, I said. How's that feel?

Hagen's hands shook like a disturbed glass of milk. Let's get the hell out of here, he said.

. . .

The rally took place the following afternoon. And as I had pre-supposed, there was little to report: maybe two hundred Klan members and neo-Nazis, and dozens of police officers required to protect them from a thousand counterprotesters. The network reporters were done up in their pancake makeup despite the humidity, broadcasting from director's chairs underneath portable awnings.

Klan organizers had neglected to bring microphones or amplifiers and so the "rally" was little more than a mimed minstrel show of white supremacists strutting about the steps of the statehouse like a cartload of chimpanzees, squalling and scratching themselves and shouting racial epithets nobody could quite make out.

Hagen stood imperious and motionless, stage left, playing every bit the Grand Dragon. His old man, a former Texas Klansman, would have been proud. Simpson stood nearby with his hand raised in a White Power salute.

These were people to fear, no doubt, and in the case of individual men like Roof, homicidal maniacs who needed to be hunted down and jailed. But it was clear to me that the Klan was a fringe, bereft of a philosophy or followers or the intellect required to commit anything more than isolated one-man acts of terror. The Grand Dragon may have been supporting Trump, and there were no doubt other racists and misogynists attracted to him, but the foundation of white discontentment and the reasons for it lay elsewhere in America, beyond this clan of baboons.

After an hour of shouting themselves purple, the Klan was ordered by the authorities to clear off the capitol steps. A contingent of the Bloods street gang took the opportunity to snatch the Klansmen's banners, pelt them with bottles, and chase them off into a parking garage. One white supremacist ran straight into a light pole and broke his nose. I looked hard, but Hagen and Simpson had slipped away.

I don't know whatever became of Simpson or if he's managed to find steady employment. As for Hagen, he stayed busy. Over the course of the following year, he was charged with assault with a deadly weapon after impaling a Latino protester with an American flagpole at a violent "White Lives Matter" rally he'd organized in Anaheim, California. In a separate incident, he was arrested and charged for the multiple stabbing and attempted murder of a fellow Klansman during a boozy evening at the North Carolina home of the Imperial Wizard, reportedly over an argument about who among them was most racist.

*A mad mania had gripped the globe. Its daily cycle began pumping at approximately 10 a.m. local time in the editorial conference rooms across the planet. The meetings would begin with the same question: Did Trump say or tweet anything outrageous this morning?*

*The editorial staffs, regardless of their political vantage point, couldn't get enough of the man they universally despised. This Orange Oaf was a danger to the status quo. And the status quo, of course, was largely composed of those self-important types sitting around the editorial tables, for whom he had no respect.*

*The more the media establishment tittered, harangued, lectured, gasped, finger-wagged, the more ordinary Americans were drawn to Trump. And the ordinary Americans who were repulsed by him couldn't help but stare. Just three months into the race, Trump looked like the pick, as I'd told him when he held a rally in suburban Flint several weeks earlier.*

*The glass was half-empty in America. Less than half of American households were now considered middle class, and half the middle-class wealth had evaporated during the Great Recession. Rent was eating half their paychecks. This was not of their doing, or at least they didn't think so. It was the establishment who had raped them.*

*The American Redneck was in full mutiny against his Republican master. He was not in the mood for gentlemanly debate or shrinking violets. He was angry and broke or close to it.*

*The only thing people despised more than the reporters were the politicians and bankers. And they wanted them all punched in the mouth. Fuck it if Trump didn't know what he was talking about. Kick 'em in the balls, Donny boy!*

*Even Bernie Sanders, the curmudgeonly socialist from the hills of Vermont, was making a run of it against Hillary Clinton. And all the Bern had to do was take some windmill slaps at faceless billionaires, call for the return of Depression-era bank regulations, say no to global trade deals, and promise college to everybody without explaining how we were going to pay for it. It almost worked. Except the establishment had laid facedown, ass up for Clinton. She had the money and the superdelegates and the friends at the TV networks. Bern didn't get the coverage—good or bad. He was disheveled, puckered, professorial, elderly. The camera didn't like him.*

*Trump was a different duck. Whenever he would lie, exaggerate, mock, threaten, or compare a fellow Republican to a child molester, the captains of the sinking media ships would notice a bounce in their click count and ratings. Business was business. The boat was afloat. So they made a conscious decision to turn it into the Donald Trump Show.*

*To me, Trump rated as a prop. The lipstick and panty hose on the pig. The backdrop. He was important, no doubt, but we would not castigate him, just bat him around like a ball of yarn. We weren't campaign beat reporters. We were street reporters. In our view, the story was and always will be the American people scratching it out from Ferguson to Flint. Certainly there was room for this in the vomit of continual political coverage.*

*So I thought.*

# My Blue Hell

The set for the Republican debate at the Reagan Library was a predictable blue. TV news sets in America are universally blue. Electric lapis. Deep azure. Ocean breeze. Aqua Viagra.

Blue, no matter the tonality, secretes a certain gravitas, authority, power. At least that's what the TV set designers tell network executives who are not known for their originality.

Then again, there are only two national TV news set designers in America. There used to be just one, but the principals of that design firm split a decade ago and now there were two set design firms pimping the same vapid blue fish tank, accentuated by the occasional streak of crimson. Blue sets give me a disorienting vibe of cyanopsia, a condition of seeing things tinted in blue—a common side effect of overdosing on erectile pills.

As if to complete the erection motif, the designer of the evening's set had built three stories of scaffolding so that the podiums of the eleven Republican contenders would be level with the wings of the Gipper's old Air Force One jetliner on permanent display at the library. A gigantic silver dildo as a backdrop. The plane was meant to symbolize something, I don't know what.

Just ten weeks after announcing his candidacy, Trump was in command not only of the polls, but the media. The guy had shocked the establishment and they despised his disregard for their rules, but he was ratings gold for a catatonic industry whose viewers were fleeing in droves. Twenty-four million people had tuned in to watch the Big Orange insult everybody during the previous debate. Seeing that, the network televising this contest was doubling down on the game show motif and increasing its ad buys by 40 percent. Cha-ching!

It is easy to posture with a certain earnestness and idealism about the political process, but under the strain for ratings, these principles are the first casualties. The debate started like this:

INTRO: (Sweeping overhead shot. Host in foreground with blue
    suit and red tie, his back to the contestants who are jammed
    together like discount shoe shoppers. Jet plane far in back-
    ground. Red carpet, blue tones.)
HOST: The eleven leading Republican candidates for president
    are at their podiums. They're ready to face off. And if you've
    been watching this race, you know, anything could happen
    over the next few hours! . . . Now, let's begin!

After a few opening comments, the host sets them up like pugilists, hoping somebody is going to pull a Mike Tyson and bite off a chunk of his opponent's ear.

HOST: Would you feel comfortable with Donald Trump's finger on the nuclear codes?

SEN. RAND PAUL: I'm very concerned about him—having him in charge of the nuclear weapons, because I think his response, his—his visceral response to attack people on their appearance—short, tall, fat, ugly—my goodness, that happened in junior high. Are we not way above that? Would we not all be worried to have someone like that in charge of the nuclear arsenal? (*Applause*)

HOST: Mr. Trump?

DONALD TRUMP: I never attacked him on his look, and believe me, there's plenty of subject matter there. (*Laughter*)

The print press was off in the side tent watching on the Jumbotron, banging away on their keyboards, rocking to and fro like a troop of Rhesus monkeys* attempting to augur the sequence that releases the banana chip, compiling the best zingers of the night.

*Booyah! That one makes the list!* I felt bad for them. By the time their stories were posted, the debate would be over and the talking heads would be frothing like a bottle of rancid wine and by then nobody would read their blogs. Who were they writing for? I wondered. Did they know nobody was reading?

But of course they were reading, this was Trump. Subscriptions were up. The guy was going to save all our jobs.

We had been in Southern California for a few days and already had the bulk of our story in the can. Though the subject didn't rate more than twenty minutes in the three-hour debate,

---

* Primate research has shown that such behavior is symptomatic of the onset of insanity brought about by the deprivation of meaningful sensory stimulation.

our story from California was not the debate, but rather immigration.

One million people living in Los Angeles County were without legal documentation. The majority of them were Mexican. In fact, one man we interviewed mopping the Gipper's grave told us he had come illegally from Mexico a dozen years earlier. Many of the men on the grounds crew who tended the corpse of Reagan were from Central America and had fled Reagan's proxy wars there back in the '80s, only to be granted amnesty by Reagan himself. Before we could conduct deeper interviews with the grounds crew, security came and shooed us away.

Trump and the other candidates were talking about the feasibility of building a wall on the Mexican border. New Jersey governor Chris Christie did one better, suggesting we put bar codes on immigrants so we could track them like packages. All of it was bullshit. There was no money for a wall, and international treaty forbade building one along the Rio Grande, anyway. And someone needed to point out to Governor Christie that people have legs, packages don't.

Then there was the matter of rounding up grandmothers in greater Los Angeles. It would only serve to incite a riot, Deputy Chief Jose Perez of the Los Angeles Police Department told me. Besides, where would we hold *abuela* while she was awaiting the bus ride home? We had no place to put the children we were catching on the Texas border, for that matter.

Our story from Los Angeles asked a simple question: Why not start with something most Americans agree on. Why not run out the three-quarters of a million illegal aliens who had been convicted of violent crimes? Why not legally compel so-called "sanctuary cities" to cooperate with the federal authorities in identifying these people?

Take the sad life of Jamiel Shaw, who watched his son die on his own street corner in South Central Los Angeles. A high school football star and honors student, seventeen-year-old Jamiel Jr. was gunned down by a gang-banger who was in the country illegally, after the gang-banger mistook Jamiel Jr. for a member of the rival Bloods street gang because he was carrying a red Spider-Man book bag.

The killer was a suspect in three prior murders and had been released from the county jail just the day before, where he'd been serving time on a weapons charge. Immigration officials were not notified of his release. And what's more, Los Angeles's Special Order 40 forbids police from checking the immigration status of known criminals or suspects.

Shaw wept bitterly as we spoke at the scene of his son's murder, a plaque marking the spot not a hundred yards from his home.

What was the guy doing here? Shaw wanted to know. Why can't we get these people out of here? Because he has rights? Didn't my son have a right to grow into a man? Didn't he?

A recent poll by the University of California at Berkeley showed that people overwhelmingly agreed with Shaw about sanctuary cities. Among those people was Alfonso Fernandez, an undocumented day laborer at the Home Depot in Hollywood.

The criminals are no good, he said. They make problems. They steal from us. Every week, we have to pay the gangs to be here. You don't pay, you have problems.

The intellectual justification for sanctuary cities and Special Order 40 is that the protection they provide encourages illegal immigrants to cooperate with law enforcement authorities without fear they'll be deported. But if that was the case, then why weren't men at the Home Depot informing the cops about the pukes and shakedown artists preying on them?

Are you *loco, señor*? is the answer I got.

. . .

There was also nothing said in the debate about what to do with the three-quarters of a million farm workers who make less than the federal minimum wage, but do one of the most important jobs for Americans. They feed us.

For one hundred years, these have been Mexican jobs because American farmers have always been addicted to cheap labor. And the arrangement has been good for all concerned. Why not legitimize the workers with a '"Blue Card"—an agricultural work permit? Maybe this way, Daniel, a grape picker in the San Joaquin Valley and the father of three American-born children, could have returned to Mexico for his mother's funeral. Why not free him from these petty indignities?

As far as I knew, the only referendum ever held on illegal immigrants occurred in California two decades earlier. Proposition 187 would have established a statewide screening system that would have prevented the undocumented from receiving public money, health care, and education. It passed easily in liberal California but was eventually struck down by the courts. The most interesting thing about the referendum was the racial breakdown of those who voted for it: 63 percent of whites, 58 percent of blacks, 58 percent of Asians, and 31 percent of Latinos. Americans and their view of immigration was much more complex than the TV debates and news segments were presenting.

Immigration. This was the true subject of our California story. The debate was simply cellophane wrap to us. A couple of empty calories to fold into the dough.

Swept away in the post-debate media scrum, we waited respectfully as our colleague from the *Access Hollywood* think tank asked Trump about his facial expressions and soul-brother handshakes.

Sensing an opening, I slid my question in while clutching Trump's jacket tails.


ME: Why don't we get the Mexicans to build the Wall on their
    side? That way everybody at the Home Depot will run home
    to build it and seal themselves in!
TRUMP: Yeah, and Mexico's gonna pay for it.
ME: Awesome!


Senator Lindsey Graham, who statistically may have been drawing negative votes, was still hanging around, all five foot seven of him, talking tough.

What about the violent illegals? I asked. Shouldn't we focus on them?

We need to kick their asses, the little guy snarled.

The nonsense. The platitudes. The starched collars. The soft-handed politicians talking like gunslingers. It was too much, and I spontaneously snatched Matt's lapels and we do-si-do'd, spinning around the spin room. I'm told we appeared in the background on every major cable network. My mom called to say hello. But it did not go over well with the executives.

I thought everybody knew this was a sock puppet show. But apparently I wasn't showing the process proper reverence. *This is our country. This is the highest office in the free world. Give it the proper respect.*

Respect? The promo commercials had called the debate Round 2: The Main Event, and even dubbed in the preposterous chiming of a prizefight bell. It was sold as Rocky Balboa meets *Family Feud.*

To me, the spin room was no better, nothing more than a powder room of empty parlor talk. This was TV journalism, and I was guilty of running down the long plastic hallway and urinating on the carpet.

I thought back to that Kennedy-Nixon debate of 1960: We'd gone from two men trying to avoid makeup to ten men wearing more makeup than their female rival. We'd gone from two chairs and a drab gray background to a Hollywood set lit in boner-pill blue and a silver jet plane. Americans knew what time it was and I thought I was doing them the proper job.

I don't know if the spin-room spinning was the last straw. It could have been, but maybe it was New York. A few weeks earlier, we had done a story on the seeming unwinding of New York City. Like in a lot of urban centers in America, murder there was up and bums were bathing in public fountains. But in the Big Apple they had the additional scourge of costumed cartoon characters and topless women wandering around Times Square posing for pictures for tips. Sometimes Elmo and Batman were arrested for pushing kids to the ground or groping women. Sometimes the topless chicks were busted for turning tricks. If you believed the *New York Post* headlines, it was the end of times. Naked chicks!

In the course of interviewing the topless women being topless myself, I received an alert that Trump was giving a press conference at Trump Tower just a few blocks away that very afternoon. He was going to sign the Republican loyalty pledge. Now all seventeen hopefuls—including Trump—would agree to support the party's eventual nominee. No third-party candidates. One big happy family. It was bullshit, of course. Nobody in politics keeps his word. Another media stunt. Still, a Trump cameo always boosts ratings. So we headed over to Fifth Avenue.

Security was heavy. The media crowd was huge, taking up half the lobby. We weren't on the list. Not to worry.

NEWS MEDIA PRESS OFFICIAL IDENTIFICATION.

Worked like a charm. And we were waved in.

We waited and waited for the political media to talk itself blue about the pledge. Then *Access Hollywood* got its turn asking about rapper Kanye West's threat to run for president.

Don loved Kanye.

Someone else asked about New England Patriots quarterback Tom Brady and the playoff-game Deflategate scandal. Don was happy to entertain the questions. Don loved Tom.

Then he called on me.

Sir, the naked women in Times Square, I asked. Where do you stand on that?

His brow crinkled. I don't want to talk about that, he grumbled. It's inappropriate.

Snickers from the media again.

Inappropriate? The American urban center was spinning off its axis. There were riots and marches and poverty and bums in the birdbaths. You want to lead the country, then you have to know where to begin. That starts with knowing what's going on outside our window. Inappropriate? Cool with me. I can write to that.

I had TV gold in my hand. I had America wrapped up in topless chicks. I had Batman calling them prostitutes. I had Tangerine Trump.

The call from the executives came after the Los Angeles piece aired. No more Trump, they ordered. No more spinning in the spin room. The local TV executives around the country did not appreciate it.

How was I to know I was supposed to take the shitshow seriously? What with the gigantic aluminum dildo as a backdrop and a

five-foot senator threating to beat Mexican gangster ass? This
wasn't New York's or Los Angeles's or D.C.'s election. It was ours,
out here in the moldering middle, a place apparently impossible to
see from the coastal corridors of power or the skyscraper canyons
where the media elite resided. This election didn't belong to the
suits. It belonged to the flannel. But orders are orders and I was being shipped back to the minor leagues. The serious girls and boys of
TV news would handle the national politics.

I also received a call from accounting over my New York ex-
penses, questioning a dinner receipt I had submitted, which consisted of nine pints of beer and a plate of calamari.

Guilty as charged. But you've got to oil a pimp somehow, I tried
to explain. Sources want drinks, not baked ziti. And beer is cheaper
than a New York strip steak that I was entitled to if I had wanted it.

No booze on the tab, period, I was informed. Company policy.

And just like that, I was grounded until further review of previous expense forms. No more traveling. No more America.

You'd have thought I'd hacked into Prince Harry's cell phone.

*Just a few days before Trump was to announce his candidacy, I ran down and tackled a twenty-year-old black man named Orlando Thomas after he had mugged a friend of mine and stolen her cell phone.*

*There I was, trying my damnedest to keep this two-hundred-pound man pinned to the pavement in the middle of a busy down-town intersection during lunch rush. He threatened to kill me if he got loose. I hadn't considered that possibility until he brought it up.*

*We were just three blocks from police headquarters, but a squad car wouldn't arrive for the better part of twenty minutes. Apparently, in the "new" Detroit, the apprehension of a strong-arm bandit who was flailing away in the middle of two-way traffic was not a high priority.*

*After some time, an FBI agent on his lunch break sauntered up with a set of slip-knot handcuffs jerry-rigged from a pair of shoe-laces. As I struggled with Thomas, I wondered where the agent got the laces. He was wearing loafers.*

*Upset that he had threatened my life, I whispered into Thomas's ear that I promised he would do time. He had a tattoo on his left forearm of dice and flames. You just crapped out, motherfucker, I whispered in his ear.*

*And so now we were in district court awaiting his arraignment. Me the witness. He the defendant. The guy was a habitual criminal, a three-striker with convictions for breaking and entering, larceny, and robbery who had done no real jail time. In the revolving-door system of the Detroit criminal justice system, he had always been given probation and ordered to pay court costs. He would neglect the court costs, violate his probation, and promptly commit a new crime, only to receive probation and court costs again. That's how it goes in America. The jails and prisons were overflowing with young black men. There was no room for attempted murderers and felons in possession of illegal firearms, much less this guy. That's why a shit-for-brains like Thomas was left free to prey on people after the briefest stays in the jailhouse.*

*But not this time. Not the fourth time. I'd made Thomas that promise. Welcome to the shitshow, son.*

*The judge was a swell enough guy. He recognized me from TV and wished me good morning. And then his clerk emerged from chambers like a high-end manservant carrying a tray containing danish and a sweating decanter of ice water. The only thing missing was the white gloves.*

*The judge nodded appreciatively toward me and smiled sweetly. Go ahead, help yourself.*

*I got the feeling the judge knew that I knew that he was the one responsible for Thomas's most recent probation release and didn't want me shaking out the sheets, and hanging him up to dry on the ten o'clock news. The strawberry strudel being dangled before me seemed to affirm that.*

*Mr. LeDuff, would you like some water?*

*No thank you, Your Honor.*

*Some pastry, then? It's really quite delicious.*

*No thank you.*

*The citizens seated in the galley, beaten down by an unresponsive and often unfair bureaucracy, marveled at the dignity provided me. They, of course, were offered nothing.*

*The Motor City really was little different from Chicago or Baltimore or Philadelphia. The focus was on the shiny new downtown buildings, while beneath it all the foundations of the civic endeavor were crumbling.*

*Thomas was sentenced to three to fifteen years in prison. Before being taken away, he struggled with the bailiffs, shouted ungracious things about my mother while strongly suggesting I take some time to pleasure myself. I had to laugh, imagining him telling the boys on the cellblock that he was doing a three-year minimum over a purple cell phone. I laughed until I walked outside the courthouse doors.*

*Across the street was a $200 million pile of rubble that was supposed to be the new county jail complex—that is until I exposed it a few years earlier as a swamp of incompetence and cronyism. There had been no master blueprint or budget for the proposed building. What there had been was plenty of money for connected Republican contractors who in turn contributed to the Democratic county political bosses who pushed the unnecessary and unaffordable project through. Once we had exposed this, construction ground to a halt.*

*What was left—what I was staring at—was a mockery: stanchions to nowhere, cellblocks exposed to the elements, weeds and gravel and dust. Imagine what might have been done for the citizens with that $200 million (plus interest)?*

*Nobody had gone to prison for this outrage. It was lunchtime at that very hour, and I imagined every silk suit associated with this stinking deal eating steak somewhere, laughing it up over a glass of Bordeaux.*

*Meanwhile, dipshit Orlando Thomas was getting a baloney sandwich, a box of milk, and a one-way ride to the state penitentiary.*

# Brass Balls

I was in bed, perusing the thinning Sunday paper. Buried inside was another glowing story about the demolitions in Detroit. The U.S. Department of the Treasury was to send more than a quarter billion dollars in leftover federal mortgage bailout money for homeowners so the city could tear down some of the forty thousand abandoned houses.

Detroit's blight had become famous since the global economic collapse. Tourists came to romp in its enormity. For those who lived within it, the blight was a cancer, pulling down the spirit and the health of the citizens.

With each successive story, the reported number of demolished houses kept changing. First it was four thousand houses, and then it would be six thousand houses, and then five thousand houses.

It made me curious. Tethered to my professional restraining collar and grounded in Detroit, Michigan, I decided to do some digging in my own backyard. What I found was arithmetical alchemy. More than half the time, the lowest bidder wasn't awarded the contracts and the price of demolitions had ballooned 50 percent since the last mayor, Dave Bing, a former NBA great known more for his jump shot than his managerial competence.

And who was the self-admitted mastermind of this boondoggle? Mayor Mike Duggan.

I wasn't surprised. The citizens didn't really know who they had elected. The press, preoccupied with the bankruptcy, never truly vetted him. The people still called him *DOO-gan* when it was actually pronounced *DUH-gan*—exactly the same pronunciation as Patrick J. Duggan, a federal court judge who also happened to be the mayor's father. The elder Duggan had undoubtedly proved a helpful connection in the ambitious and troubled political career of the son.

Wherever Mike Duggan went, the feds seemed to follow. And yet nothing ever stuck. Accusations of graft and no-bid contracts at Detroit Metropolitan Airport dogged his administration when he was deputy county executive. His boss, Wayne County Executive Ed McNamara, died in the middle of the federal probe into the airport, but by then Duggan had moved on, unscathed, to become county prosecutor. But not for long. Campaign finance irregularities, a grand jury investigation, and more no-bid contracts may have been contributing reasons as to why he resigned his post prematurely.

He was then named by Governor Jennifer Granholm (also a product of the McNamara machine) as the head of the financially struggling Detroit Medical Center complex. With no hospital executive experience, Duggan would eventually broker the sale of the facilities to a for-profit health-care company, but not before the Duggan-led DMC was fined $30 million by the federal government for fraud and kickbacks. Even so, Duggan, the Teflon Leprechaun, got a $2 million payout and moved on.

Detroit was desperate for a new start, and compared to his opponent, Sheriff Benny Napoleon—who himself had been caught up in the county jail scandal—Duggan appeared the fresher of two soiled socks.

Now here we were again—more problems with the public's money.

After my first story on the demolition irregularities hit, Duggan convened a dog and pony show with the city council. I was not invited, but I showed anyway. Hizzoner explained to the council that the cost overruns were simply a matter of inflation and the price of good, clean dirt to fill the holes where houses once stood. He also said the program's problems had been inflated by the media—me—and the next time I came knocking, Duggan promised he would handle me himself.

That's when I got a call from a man named Barry Ellentuck, who had served as the chief of demolition for Mayor Bing. Ellentuck, a short, bald power lifter from New Jersey, had been hired by the state of Michigan to monitor the federal money being funneled through it to the city of Detroit and Duggan. He told me he had information I might be interested in.

We met in a dank contractor's garage, in a shattered corner of the city where the grass went unmowed and the potholes unpatched. Ellentuck handed me a thumb drive that contained a raft of documents and email exchanges, which showed what appeared to be collusion and price fixing between a small group of contractors and the mayor's handpicked executives.

I called the mayor and was summoned to his office a few days later. I laid out the documents on his conference table and, implausibly, Duggan admitted—on camera—that he had indeed instructed his men to negotiate a preset price with a handpicked group of contractors, many of whom had made political contributions to him. In the end, those handpicked contractors with inside information won the work at inflated prices they had established themselves.

Graft goes on everywhere in America. Remember that the New Orleans mayor went to prison for padding his pockets with Hurricane Katrina money. Remember that four out of the previous seven Illinois governors had been sent to prison for corruption. Remember that in Albany, New York, the state legislature was perpetually cranking out turds of political putrefaction, and the leaders of both the state senate and assembly were at that very moment being convicted of corruption and sent to prison. (One conviction was later vacated and the other was overturned.)

But Detroit was special. Maybe I was biased because this was my hometown. Or maybe I was outraged because the Motor City was all the way broke and the federal government had sent life-altering money to clean up the neighborhoods where the most destitute children in urban America lived: children who routinely played in fetid piles of the rotting housing stock. It's worth remembering that former mayor Kwame Kilpatrick was doing the better part of three decades in the federal pen, for, among other things, swinging contracts. And Kilpatrick wasn't even the first Detroit mayor to go to prison. I reminded Duggan of all this.

He reacted like a cornered opossum. He snarled, calling my stories lies. He hissed, threatening multiple times over the course of the next weeks to sue me for defamation because I had called his demolition executives "overpaid minions" who "couldn't even manage a candy store." He curled up in a ball and played dead, refusing follow-up interviews with me and demanding that all questions be put in writing. City hall mocked me on Facebook and the city's official web page. Basically, the mayor of Detroit pulled a Trump before Trump pulled a Trump, and my bosses got worried. Fake news!

Any further luncheon dates with Hizzoner were out of the question.

Ellentuck called me a few days after another of these stories aired, saying a reporter at the *Free Press* was calling, wanting to see the emails himself.

What should I do? he asked.

Give him everything, I said.

Normally it was the TV that cannibalized the newspapers' work, without attribution. I thought I was doing my company a solid by having a competitor vet the story, because nobody else in the local press wanted to touch it. No one wanted to dump on Detroit. It didn't fit the narrative of the Comeback City.

But was it a comeback? In the neighborhoods where black people lived, unemployment was too high and property values were too low. Violent crime was through the roof. Thousands of families were being tossed from their homes due to tax foreclosures. Those homes were being stripped of anything worth stealing by scrappers, and more houses appeared on the demolition lists. And of course, those demolition prices had exploded, making it impossible for the neighborhoods to tread water.

Give the newspaper reporter the documents you gave me, I told Ellentuck, because if this played out like I thought it would, yet another Detroit mayor would—or at least could—be indicted.

A month or so later, the story landed in the *Free Press:* "City officials and handpicked companies agreed to a contract price for a massive project before others could submit bids."

. . .

Ellentuck had brass balls, but even brass balls get crushed under the weight and power of the Machine. The day following
the newspaper story, like a lightning bolt, the attorney general of
the state of Michigan charged Ellentuck himself with fraud, of attempting to overbill the city demolition program by $6,000 during
his role as the assessor of the program.

Never mind that millions of federal dollars had evaporated
without a wisp of a paper trail. Or that the air the children breathed
was poisoned with asbestos and lead as a consequence of the subpar
demolitions. The mayor wasn't getting charged by the AG. It was
the whistleblower who was taking it on the chin.

It reeked of a political hit.

I was called into the boss's office. He carried the awful look of a
man who'd swallowed sour milk. And why wouldn't he? He'd received a gleeful email from Duggan's lawyer after the announce-
ment of Ellentuck's charges—reiterating their demand for a
retraction and an apology for defaming the mayor's men. How far
did the mayor's tentacles reach?

Let's lay off the mayor for a while, the boss said. And who could
blame him? Whoever heard of a public official suing the press for
holding his feet to the fire? It was outrageous. It was unconstitu-
tional. And it worked.


Ten months later, the mayor would convene a press conference
in which he would admit that his minions could not manage a
candy store. The state-of-the-art demolition program he'd so loudly
crowed about had been quietly shut down by the feds for two

months, during which time the "improper billing" of millions of federal dollars had been uncovered by investigators.

All of this had been supervised by the minions. The mayor himself was shocked! shocked! to hear of the dirty deeds. The mayor announced one minion had resigned. The minion told me later that he'd been fired. He also told me he took direct orders from the mayor.

2016

# Yellow Water

The Kirkwood mobile home park was now a ghost town. The trailer homes were blown out. The windows and door of unit 1521 were wide open, a curtain billowing in the wind. In front of unit 1500 was a moldering heap of the previous tenant's belongings and a dead dog in a plastic bag. Unit 1420 had had its aluminum siding stripped for scrap, its exposed studs and insulation giving it the look of a gigantic hay bale. A feral cat skulked beneath it. The trailer park had been foreclosed on for back taxes and shuttered, the people pushed to the wind. When a last-chance trailer park closes down, you know the end of times is upon you.

Forbidden to travel the country, to poke Don the Orange, to kick Mike the White, I returned to Flint to find the red-toothed people who a year and a half ago were mixing the tap water with Kool-Aid and white sugar to make it go down. The government at all levels had assured them that despite the smell and "cosmetic" flaws in the water then being drawn from the Flint River, it was safe to drink.

Now it turned out to be a damnable lie. The government had

known for some time and now the governor was forced to admit it: Flint and its babies had been poisoned. Happy New Year, Vehicle City. Where had you gone, Dee Johnson?

The untreated river water had caused an estimated fifteen to twenty thousand service lines to corrode, leaching toxic lead into the tap water. The issue of yellow water had been brewing for two years. The state and local government were covering up tests that showed lead poisoning. The studies began to leak out. A local doctor found lead in the children as well. It took cable television to get the nation to give a damn. So count one for TV.

The lead wasn't even the worst of it. An outbreak of Legionnaires' disease linked to the tainted water had killed at least a dozen people in the county and infected nearly a hundred more. Turned out the state knew that too. The city knew. The county knew. The federal government knew. But the public was never told. Why?

This was big money. And if you need to know what happens to a whistleblower who inserts his principles between money and politics, all you had to do was look at the demolition scam going down in Detroit and the fate of Barry Ellentuck. Whistleblowers get crushed. Bureaucrats with tight lips stay employed.

In Flint, to make matters worse, the *Legionella* bacteria may have still been in pipes and the hot-water heaters, waiting for warm weather to begin breeding like reptiles in the sewer. People were frightened in this hardscrabble town of ninety-nine thousand, about an hour's drive north of Detroit. And still the government told them nothing.

I was ashamed. And so was Matt. We were aware of the water problems in Flint. We saw it in the Kool-Aid-stained teeth of the children. We did nothing about it. No follow-up. No stories. Instead, we drank beer and ate calamari and ran around the country doing segments on the plights of others, ignoring the suffering of our own neighbors. And now that we had come back to the trailer park to find them, they were gone.

They were gone and the officials responsible for their well-being were hiding beneath their desks.

The city's pipe inspector at the water plant wouldn't answer his phone.

The county health director wouldn't come to his door.

The new mayor, finding fame in the public health calamity, could not speak to the local press because she was busy in a meeting with yet another Hollywood star come to play humanitarian savior for a day.

The storefront office of the firm that was paid millions of dollars to make sure the water was safe was now empty, the only sign of former life a browning fern hanging from the ceiling.

To his credit, Republican governor Rick Snyder granted me a moist-eyed interview, accepting blame while assuring citizens that the water was now safe for washing and that he would indeed bathe his own grandchildren in it. To his discredit, the governor failed to acknowledge that he had no grandchildren. He also promised to drink the filtered tap water himself for thirty days, but after just five, our fearless leader got on a jet and flew off to Germany.

The irony was not lost on Tia Simpson, a thirty-one-year-old machinist who had to send away her twelve-year-old daughter, Anyja, to live with relatives when they started suffering with mysterious rashes and numbness in their extremities.

State health inspectors instructed Flint's bars and restaurants not to serve ice cubes or rinse lettuce with city water. Children and grandchildren, on the other hand? Well, go right ahead and rinse them off, the governor declared.

It's like being a leper, Simpson told me in her home, showing the brown water gurgling from her bathroom faucet. Nobody wants to touch you because they think you're contagious, because you're from Flint. And we might be. Who knows? Nobody gives a damn about us because we're poor.

For eighteen months, people drank the unfiltered water, and bathed in it and died. Nobody said anything. State employees would not drink it, having bottled water quietly ferried in. Rashes and skin lesions were apparently figments of people's imaginations. When a memo leaked from the U.S. Environmental Protection Agency citing dangerous levels of lead in Flint's water, a state spokesman denied it, telling the citizens to "relax." He has since found work with a lobbying firm in the state capital.

Finally, with the email and memo leaks, and cable television and Flint's mayor making it the news of the week, the governor was forced to declare a state of emergency in Flint.

The first of millions of bottles of clean water began arriving from the state. People were lined up in cars, their tailpipes steaming in the bitter arctic air, in front of the fire department, which was serving as a distribution center.

Yo, man! It's a joke, a middle-aged black man called to me from his car. Do the math.

So I did: One million bottles of water equaled a forty-second shower for every living soul in Flint or a two-gallon pot of soup for every household. It was a calamity beyond proportion, and here was the government, like a little boy trying to stick his finger in the dike. The malignancy of greed had metastasized into something approaching murder. Flint was now one gigantic crime scene.

It was easy—too simple, really—to blame Governor Snyder for this man-made catastrophe, though he did deserve much of the blame. Flint was the consequence of his bookish managerial style, his insistence that we could remake government with a collective focus on "relentless positive action" borrowed from his time in corporate America.

And it was Snyder who stripped Flint's mayor and city council members of power and replaced them with a string of emergency managers who had absolute authority over the city's finances and political decisions. It was Snyder's emergency manager who, in a cost-saving measure, decided to go off the Detroit water system and pipe in water from the notoriously polluted Flint River instead.

Snyder knew early on that the water was ugly. Everybody knew the water was ugly. *E. coli* and methane and boil notices and mysterious rashes. Michigan officials began quietly trucking in that purified water for a state building in Flint. After six months, General Motors, noticing rusted parts, switched its plant back to using Detroit water.

The Flint city council soon voted to do the same, but the vote was ceremonial. The city council had no real influence anymore. The city was being managed by a revolving door of operators, something like a municipal bus line. Jerry Ambrose—Flint's fourth emergency manager in three years—vetoed the resolution, calling it financially "incomprehensible."

In fairness, Flint has a long history of the financially incomprehensible. Back in 2002, hollowed out by three decades of industrial decline, the city had a $30 million operating deficit. The mayor was recalled, and then-governor Jennifer Granholm installed—you guessed it—an emergency financial manager. The books were eventually balanced and power returned to elected officials. But those elected officials turned around and blew a new $10 million hole in the budget. The new mayor, accused of bribery and lying about the city's finances, resigned for "health reasons." Enter Snyder and his band of bean counters.

All the while, it appeared that Detroit's water utility was

fleecing Flint, charging one of the poorest cities in the United States the highest water rates in the country, in a state surrounded by the world's largest pool of fresh water.

So in 2013, Flint's civic leaders pushed for the construction of their own separate $300 million water system running parallel to Detroit's. It wasn't necessary; Detroit's water was perfectly fine, if overpriced. But think of the jobs! Think of the money! Think of the political contributions! There were millions to be made off the backs of the ghetto. Think of Detroit's half-finished county jail or its demolition program.

The Chamber of Commerce wanted it. The trade unions wanted it. The local contractors wanted it. The city council rubber-stamped it. So did the mayor. And the governor's people signed off on the new multimillion-dollar water system even though Vehicle City was broke.

Who ultimately made the decision? To date, nobody in any position of power has stood up and categorically accepted responsibility, the vampire's cloak of bureaucracy shrouding every bloodsucker from the light.

I went to see one of the architects of the plan, Jeff Wright, the county drain commissioner. A wiry guy with slicked hair and a thin mustache, Wright had been an informant for the FBI during the Kilpatrick administration's Detroit water scandal in the previous decade. According to documents I had pulled, the commissioner had also raised nearly a million dollars in campaign contributions over that time while running virtually unopposed for his job. Many of those contributions came from the contractors who had been awarded work on the new water system, among them the nowhere-to-be-found firm with the dying plant hanging from the ceiling and an engineering company that also designed the now-abandoned Wayne County Jail.

I told Wright it all looked suspiciously cozy. He pointed out that all contracts were competitively bid. Just like Detroit, he said. All of this was perfectly legal, out of his control, and in the long run, the project would still save the people money, he insisted.

His answer didn't instill much confidence. Flint was poisoned. He was an FBI snitch. Detroit contracts were competitively bid, yet the mayor was in prison. Add to that the fact that Wright was drinking bottled water.

So how was the city of Flint to pay for redundant and unnecessary infrastructure when it had no money? Simple, this is America. Borrow the money. Then raise people's water bills—charging even more for the contaminated water from the Flint River than it did for the clean Detroit water. The savings to the city would be funneled back into upgrading Flint's mothballed water treatment plant.

Just one little problem here—the necessary upgrades weren't made to the old water treatment plant before people were served water from a river known as a dumping ground for corpses and car batteries. It was like flying a jet without an engine.

To review: Flint decided in 2013 to build its own parallel water system because the cost from Detroit was too high. In the meantime, while the new system was being built, the city would draw water from the Flint River and treat it. When the new system was finished in 2016, they would switch over to that new system. It was going to be perfect, until the people were poisoned.

After eighteen months of denials from Snyder's bureaucrats, and to the dismay of the architects of Flint's parallel system, Flint was finally forced back onto Detroit's water system. Tia

Simpson was still being charged for water she could not drink. Of course she was.

Flint's water crisis is a symbol that resonated across America—but a symbol of what? Of working-class decline? Disregard for a majority black population? (Flint is roughly 60 percent black, 40 percent white.) Bloated government? The push to cut and privatize public services? Scratch-my-back-development deals done with the people's money?

Was Flint an outlier or the epicenter of a Mad Max American future of crumbling roads, joblessness, and toxic water? One thing was for sure: The rage felt by the residents of Flint was little different from the rage felt in other quarters of America; the feeling that people were losing ground, that the deck was stacked against them, that the folks on top didn't care.

You know goddamn well they poisoned us and lined their own pockets while they were doing it, Simpson said. They squeezed what pennies were left out of Flint and don't care that we're sick, that we can't sell our houses. They don't care because they don't have to care. That's what it's like to be poor.

Back at the trailer park now. Standing in the hostile winter of a contaminated and dying town. Staring down at the carcass of a dead hound in an abandoned trailer park stripped of anything of value. Across the road, a brownfield where one of the world's largest factories once stood. I stood there wondering where we had lost it, wondering where the people had gone.

Threats of lawsuits from the mayor of Detroit. Complaints about calling the governor of Michigan a coward. Suddenly, I was ungrounded. But now there were expense report caveats: no beer, no direct flights, no snacks or bottled water.

Sitting in my rear office now, feeling that I was some kind of thief, I thought about how far the media business had fallen. I thought about Johnny Apple, the talented newspaperman I had known at the New York Times, who was not known for pinching the company's pennies. A veritable Pavarotti of the expense report, Apple breakfasted on poached eggs and caviar during his time on the '68 campaign trail, as he had connived for himself an unlimited travel budget. A famous story runs that Apple, while posted in Moscow, bought himself a fur coat and put it on the Times's account. His editors balked, sending back the paperwork and instructing Apple to retabulate his expense report, which, to their consternation, he did, with a note attached: Find the mink.

I thought about the stories told to me by the longtime local TV anchors who, after the eleven o'clock newscast, would order a bottle of scotch and an exotic dancer or two to blow off the day's stress. A limousine would arrive at the station to take them home.

What happened? Working in the news business today, to quote an old colleague, is like showing up to a cocktail party at one o'clock in the morning and finding all the booze gone. The bottom-line pressures brought by stockholders and the internet have stripped the *business of what glamour and vigor it ever had. At least on our level. Even as national correspondents for Fox's local TV group, we were little better than traveling brush salesmen. We were as often put up in crack-infested motels as in three-star hotels. Why the company did business with such places I can't say. Hookers worked the corner. Ghouls roamed the causeways. Rooms were crawling with bedbugs. Once in San Francisco's Mission District, figuring it was too much trouble and too expensive to ask corporate for a change of location, I sucked it up and simply wrapped my head in a towel. That may have saved my scalp, but not my scrotum.*

*I never did journalism for the perks. I do it for the adventure and curiosity and the freedom from the nine-to-five prison cell. I'm no Johnny Apple, and the old newspaperman's face would probably have puckered with disdain when he saw the most lavish expense report I'd ever submitted: nine pints of beer and a plate of calamari. It took three months for the green eyeshades to decide that I was going to pay for it. Forget that I told them three months ago that I would pay for it.*

*So, ungrounded now, off we flew on a two-stop flight to Oregon to cover the armed takeover of a bird sanctuary. The Bundy family was at it again with their guns. Risking a whiteout blizzard to make our connecting flight, we nearly skidded off the side of a mountain, blowing out a tire on the rental car.*

*I would later be told about more caveats: The company didn't pay for blown tires or funerals, either.*

# And the White Horse You Rode In On

A whiff of conspiracy had infiltrated the camp. Booda, the chief of security, had disappeared into the night.

The group of armed militiamen were muttering guardedly among themselves while I, the media, listened in on every word.

*Snitch* was the whisper around the fire.

The men who had heretofore been strangers bonded in their mutual paranoia. A twenty-four-hour sentry would have to be posted in the fire lookout tower. The feds, possibly armed with inside information, could come in guns a-blazing at any time. A militia-operated drone would be needed to surveil the open white expanse. Aerial reconnaissance was a matter of life and death.

*We might be compromised.*

*Definitely.*

*Be vigilant, brother.*

*Oohrah.*

I was back among the Bundy militia, but things weren't going as smoothly as they had in Nevada, the sense of purpose there replaced by deprivation and paranoia.

Shouting matches had erupted throughout the day, one accusing the other of being an informant for the FBI. They were low on underpants and cheese slices and coffee creamer and had called on supporters across the nation to mail these necessities to a P.O. box or bring them directly, along with their guns, to the Malheur National Wildlife Refuge. One of the militiamen had stolen the money donated by supporters and had gone off to town on a bender.

So when the strangers, cold, agitated, and cranky, turned to me for whiskey, I could offer none, as drinks were a corporate no-no. Besides, none could have helped.

These self-styled patriots, who had initially come to this barren, snow-covered corner of the Pacific Northwest to show support for a family of ranchers destined for prison after setting clearing fires to federal lands, ended up seizing the 187,000-acre bird sanctuary administered by the U.S. Fish and Wildlife Service from, well . . . nobody, really. It was the deep freeze of winter—off-season for migratory fowl watchers. And now they were stuck with no graceful way out.

The move was the latest in an ongoing range war brought on by antigovernment activists operating on the philosophy that Washington had no right to hold any lands. There were three dozen men and women here, no more, but they had brought heavy firepower: pistols, semiautomatic assault rifles, shotguns, two-way radios, binoculars.

The media too had seen their call to arms, put out via Facebook, and they arrived in gaggles, accounting for a bigger presence than the occupiers themselves. There were the satellite trucks and telescopic microphone poles, makeup kits and daily noon press briefings.

I couldn't help but feel that many of the press members were secretly hoping for another Waco or Ruby Ridge.

It was a Bundy ranch homecoming and a coming-out party all at once. The leader of the occupiers was Ammon Bundy, who had come to prominence after leading the armed standoff against federal agents at his father's Nevada ranch in 2014.

But Ammon wasn't from Oregon. He lived in suburban Phoenix. Even his daddy, Cliven, wondered aloud on public radio what business his son had taking over a bird rookery in Oregon. Defending your own home was one thing; invading another man's town was another matter altogether.

His blood father notwithstanding, Ammon believed he was being guided by the Divine Father who he believed intended these lands to be held and worked by good Christian people. And many of the old crew, emboldened by the victorious Nevada standoff, were there with him. LaVoy Finicum, the group's spokesman, wrapped in a blue tarp, rifle scabbarded across his waist, was daring someone, anyone, to come try and arrest him. There was Ryan Payne, the tense, brooding Iraq War veteran and self-proclaimed leader of the sniper corps at the Bundy ranch confrontation.

And then there was Booda, aka Brian Cavalier, the security chief, who had oozed such menace and mystery during our first encounter in Nevada. Something had happened to him. He wasn't the same braggadocious warrior—the battle-hardened Marine veteran—I'd met at the Bundy ranch. Perhaps it was the recent report by an enterprising newspaperman who had dug up Booda's military record. There was, in fact, no military record. The only citations Booda ever earned, it seemed, were for petty theft and extreme DUI. He was a fraud.

And now Booda had slipped away in the dark, either having abandoned his post or out there executing some secret maneuvers.

The men around the campfire believed him to be an informant. I figured he was just an embarrassment. He wasn't a special ops sniper; he wasn't even a Buddhist. He was just an overweight bullshit artist with bad tattoos and an inability to spell.

There was a new man in the Bundy circle: Jon Ritzheimer, an antagonistic, high-strung ex-Marine from Arizona with a shaved head. He wandered around the campfire quoting Thomas Paine, instructing the others about a nefarious and subliminal plot to make sharia the supreme law in America.

Ritzheimer, thirty-two, had become something of a YouTube phenom after posting a misty-eyed video from here to his daughters, apologizing for missing Christmas because he was in Oregon defending the United States Constitution against all enemies, foreign and domestic. It was a cinematic tour de force complete with a pocket-size Constitution, tears, breathy shudders, and dramatic pauses.

It wasn't the first time Ritzheimer had become a social media spectacle. In the past, he had posted video of himself holding armed, anti-Islam rallies at a mosque in Phoenix. There he was at a Trump rally in Mesa, Arizona, spewing anti-Islamic scatology as Trump had proposed a Muslim ban in America. There he was again, threatening to arrest a U.S. senator who voted in favor of the Iran nuclear deal. His additional credits included appearances on CNN and *The Today Show* as he drove across America brandishing a pistol as he posed for photos in front of mosques.

Ritzheimer continued to post copiously from the Oregon Occupation, including one rant against the jokers who mailed him a bag of gummy bear penis candies in lieu of the cheese slice rations he'd requested.

What the feds were dealing with in Ritzheimer, it seemed to me, was a gun-toting, pot-smoking, self-styled savant of theology,

constitutional jurisprudence, and federal land management poli-
cies. Adding to his résumé was the fact that the Marine Corps had
trained Ritzheimer to kill.

Ritzheimer was among the first to follow Ammon Bundy's call
to the federal sanctuary. Bundy, who had grown a beard and
swapped his white hat for dark, was demanding that the federal
government turn over to local jurisdiction not only the bird refuge
but the entire half of the western United States that was under its
control. He also insisted that the county sheriff provide sanctuary
to the local ranchers being sent to prison for arson of public land.
When the sheriff refused, the Bundy militia declared him an enemy
of the people.

Most townsfolk in nearby Burns had been wary of the strangers
from the get-go, but now the shit really hit the fan. The schools
were shuttered. Police presence was beefed up because gun-toting
ideologues were questioning people in grocery stores and parking
lots. Unfamiliar men with assault rifles milled about outside the
sheriff's department and courthouse. Locals, in turn, began carrying their own weapons. Signs were hung. A letter was drafted to
the occupiers: Go Home. The militiamen never asked the Paiute
Indians how they felt. If they had, they would have heard the same:
Go Home.

Suddenly, Ritzheimer, who had ingratiated himself with the militia by carrying out the dual duties of security detail and sandwich
gofer, found he wasn't so welcome at the local post office or pizza
parlor anymore. It was brutally cold and increasingly boring. His
babies were at home. His wife was back in Phoenix earning the
bread while he was up here, collecting a military disability check
(PTSD and a bad back) and defending townspeople who didn't want
his help. For this, he'd missed Christmas, Advent, and Martin Luther King Day.

We sat in his truck, where he'd filmed his teary-eyed Christmas message, the heat turned up full.

I miss my kids, he said.

Why don't you go home?

I have a duty to be here.

What duty?

The people need help to stand up to the tyranny of the federal government.

But you're not even from here and they don't want you.

I wouldn't want to abandon my brothers and sisters.

Why not? Booda did. You could go home for a little vacation. Kiss the kids. Have a late Christmas, maybe. Come back if you want.

Yeah, maybe.

They don't want you here, dude.

He looked like he could use a stiff drink, but I wasn't going to pay for it. Corporate rules and all.


These were bizarre times in America, Matt said back at the motel. We'd seen immigrants rushing the Texas border to get into a country that was poisoning its own people and pushing them off their own street corners and ranch lands. These neurotic self-professed patriots like Ritzheimer were running around looking for a reason to be, searching for an enemy that had no real face. They told boring and often untrue war stories. They tossed around snatches of misapplied constitutional quotation. They muttered around the campfire about secret government designs to seize people's guns and forcibly relocate citizens to the cities. It was cold and they'd run out of socks and hand moisturizer.

These were dangerous men, no doubt, bigoted, grandiose. Half of them were broke, had few prospects beyond bankruptcy or foreclosure on the horizon. Perhaps there was another Timothy McVeigh among them. Maybe I had been sitting in the truck with him, or around the campfire.

Unhinged violence can come from any corner of America, and it often does. While anger and distrust toward the federal government is very real in the West, this crew didn't seem to me to be the vanguard of a violent "white" revolution any more than the Klan in Carolina did. These were half-boiled potatoes sitting around a fire fueled with stolen wood. But man, they made good TV.

I don't know if my advice had any effect, but Ritzheimer drove home less than two weeks later around the same time a humiliated Booda skulked back to the camp. Good timing for Johnny. Bad timing for Booda. The very day Ritzheimer left, the feds received word from a government informant who had infiltrated the inner circle at the refuge that Bundy, Booda, Finicum, and others were driving in two trucks and on the move. The group was arrested at a rural highway roadblock—except for LaVoy Finicum, the tarp man, who jumped out of his truck shouting: You're gonna have to put a bullet through me.

The cops obliged, shooting him dead.

*LaVoy Finicum had literally asked for it, and LaVoy Finicum received it.*

*His death at the hands of law enforcement got a smattering of "White Lives Matter" chatter from his supporters, but little more. Most everyone knows if you run a police roadblock with a loaded Ruger in your pocket it's not going to work out well.*

*Finicum was an exotic white man, an electronified exception, an extreme case whose death was orchestrated by himself in concert with his courtship of the camera. But what of the others who get no media attention, those who die in the culverts and alleyways under suspicious circumstances without an army of professional gawkers looking on?*

*Since the Michael Brown shooting in Ferguson, the* Washington Post *had taken it upon itself to track down and tabulate every death by cop in the United States and the details surrounding those incidents. Few in the media knew before then that law enforcement agencies are not required to report incidents of deadly force to the FBI. Like all crime statistics in general, the reporting is voluntary and predictably woefully undercounted. The* Post's *analysis showed deadly force by police to be 250 percent higher than historically reported.*

*Another finding may surprise you. In both 2015 and 2016 about twice as many white people died at the hands of police officers as black people. In many of these cases, like the one of the suspected drunk driver in Tennessee who was shot multiple times through his rear window by a cop who jumped into his pickup bed, there was graphic video that should call to question the need for deadly force.*

*So where was the media?*

*To be clear, by any standard or measurement, blacks tend to get the shit end of the stick in America. It should not surprise anyone that blacks, who are one-fifth the population of whites, are two and a half times more likely to die at the hands of police.*

*But why the whiteout on white deaths?*

*One would suspect that the statistics would reveal that the overwhelming majority of the whites who die at the hands of police come from the shabbier side of the tracks: the poor white boy, the rough one with bad teeth and poor grammar; the rowdy one who misbehaves and fights at the bars on Saturday night, the kind who might smoke meth, is underemployed, maybe a vet or an ex-con, a product of the desperate lower classes.*

*This man has few friends in the media world because the media world is populated by the upper-class white people, decidedly liberal, who at their cocktail tables discuss the notion of white privilege. The media elite knows about white privilege because they are the embodiment of it.*

*At least they were.*

*In their minds, they have convinced themselves that they have overcome this self-paradox. Through education, intellectual magazine articles, world travel, and psychotherapy, the white elite liberals feel they are no longer privileged. They are self-aware, world savvy, self-made. They are down with the program. They're woke.*

*In the hierarchy of American life, blacks are on the bottom and whites are on top. And so the white media is down for the black man. Which is a fine thing, but that only comes around when there is a catastrophe like Katrina or Flint or a police shooting.*

*But again, what about the poor white man? The liberal white elite who have been raised with advantage but believe they have scrubbed themselves clean of it still tag the poor white as the privileged one.*

*But how could they know? They've spent no time in his living room, his corner bar, his pistol range. To them, he's a lout and a bore and a racist, and to dig any deeper is simply an exercise in inconvenience. And they seem to think he resides only in Appalachia, although he lives right under their noses, from Boston to Bakersfield.*

*So when these white men die at the hands of law enforcement, it is universally agreed upon by liberal white media types that they must have deserved it. After all, they reason, the black man is a target simply by virtue of his skin color. What possible defense could a white man muster? Police do not kill white people, with all their privilege, unless they had it coming.*

*The elite black media hops on board—or rather turns their heads away—as they too have had little contact with the white lower class. Their interests lie more in maintaining their credibility within the struggling black community—to which they no longer belong, if they ever did.*

*Studies show what you should already know—regardless of race, people are more violent the poorer they are. The more violent and poor they are, the more contact they're likely to have with the cops.*

*There is a class issue in America, but the media seems determined to see only in stereotype and skin tone.*

# Die Whitey Die

By the time spring rolled around, the elite whites of the Republican establishment had been informed that they were being divorced. Their spouse: the working-class whites of the party who realized they'd been lied to and were leaving.

Trump was now the choice of these folks, his nomination a matter of formality. The establishment whites reacted as jilted lovers usually do: They pouted, mocked, scorned. They told the bastard to die.

In an attempt to explain the populist appeal of Trump, two conservative writers from august conservative magazines bickered over their keyboards about an imaginary "working-class" white man named Mike who had been cobbled together from a grab bag of stereotypes and clichés.

Make-Believe-Mike lived in the real-life working-class hamlet of Garbutt, located in upstate New York about twenty miles south of Rochester. He was described as an OxyContin junkie, deadbeat dad who was pulling a fraudulent Social Security check from Uncle Sam. Mike, one writer argued, needed to rent a U-Haul and move to the gas fields where there was work.

*The truth about these dysfunctional, downscale communities is that they deserve to die. Economically, they are negative assets. Morally, they are indefensible.*

The anthropologist who typed that, it should be pointed out, doubled as a Manhattan theater critic. It should also be noted that Manhattan and Garbutt are both located in New York State. If the man really cared, he could have taken the Amtrak to Garbutt to see for himself. But he didn't. At least Senator Rand Paul rode through the smoke of Baltimore, even if he never did look up.

So we drove to Garbutt, looking for a real-life Mike. Imagine that. On the hunt for a real-life working-class white person—defined as someone without a bachelor's degree. I knew it wouldn't be hard since they made up half the Republican Party and 40 percent of the country. Garbutt is one of those four-corners places: a stop sign, a few houses with peeling paint, a river, railroad tracks, and a dead gypsum mine. The place is so small there is no census data available. The people here work, or used to work, in the factories in and around Rochester.

After knocking on the town's few doors, we quickly realized that there was no Mike who lived in Garbutt. The last Mike had moved away some time ago. His son Kevin still lived there. But Mike was long gone.

Kevin Carey, fifty, was a simple guy who was tidying up his house before he went off to his nursing job at the county hospital. The house was nothing fancy, had no real womanly touches, but the refrigerator and toilet were clean. His wife had left some time ago, and Carey had raised his boy since infancy. He pulled no government subsidies or child support checks, did not do drugs or point guns at police. He didn't even keep beer in the fridge.

Carey had a second job as a private-duty nurse. Put that gig and the county hospital job together and they still didn't pay like Delco used to pay when he worked the line making windshield-wiper motors. That's what both Carey's grandfathers did, as well as his father, the last Mike from Garbutt. And that's what Carey did, until seven years ago after the company was sold and the jobs eventually got shipped off to Mexico. It was like that all over upstate New York. Thanks to the international trade deals, hundreds of thousands of well-paying factory jobs went overseas: Bausch & Lomb, Kodak, Corning, Xerox.

Carey drove an older-model truck and the house could have used a coat of fresh paint. But those were luxuries. Junior needed track shoes.

The kids at school wondered about Junior. When he graduated, he said he wanted to join the military.

Serve my country, is how Junior put it. Not very many people in my school want to do it. I just want to serve my country, be a little different.

His father preferred the boy to first go to college for a year or two. Have something to fall back on in case another man-made economic tsunami crashed over him, leaving him, like his father, dripping wet in his Indonesian-made underpants ripped down to his ankles.

I admire my dad and I look up to him, Junior told me. Coming from a factory job and going into nursing at his age. Raising me.

I showed the magazine article about Mike from Garbutt to Kevin from Garbutt. He had not seen it since they don't sell those sorts of magazines at the local grocer. They didn't have theater

critics around here either. Carey was genuinely amused about the
last few sentences.

*The white American underclass is in thrall to a vicious, selfish cul-*
*ture whose main products are misery and used heroin needles. Donald*
*Trump's speeches make them feel good. So does OxyContin . . . They*
*need real opportunity, which means that they need real change, which*
*means that they need U-Haul.*

*If you want to live, get out of Garbutt.*

Interestingly, Purdue Pharma, the manufacturers of OxyContin, who made tens of billions of dollars on a pill that narcotized
America, pleaded guilty in 2007 and paid a fine of $635 million for
lying about the addictive qualities of the "miracle" opioid. Since
then, the pharmaceutical industry has spent more than $880 mil-
lion on lobbying and campaign contributions to keep the drug and
others like them legal and flowing. The vast majority of those contributions went to conservative Republicans. At the same time, opioid overdoses have claimed more than 150,000 American lives.

Purdue Pharma, which is wholly owned by the Sackler family,
also happens to be headquartered in Stamford, Connecticut,
the hometown of the conservative magazine's founder, William
F. Buckley.

Wow, Carey said, setting the article down. Tell the writer he
doesn't have to worry about it, the young people are already moving away.

Like Denison, Iowa, it seemed the greatest export from Garbutt
was its children.

T heater critics aside, high-minded commentators call the situation of people living on the downside "respectable poverty."
But they know nothing of suddenly being tossed in the street after

generations of steady employment making windshield-wiper motors, or the family and community falling apart because of it. The people who did those jobs believed that if they worked hard, the work would always be there.

Then comes the ignominy of sitting in a night class with people half your age and having to leave early to get to the new underpaying job you once held as a teenager. You get home and the stack of bills as big and imposing as the Holy Bible mocks you from the table near the mudroom where you take your boots off.

Wages might have gone down or stagnated because of jobs flowing out of the country and cheap labor pouring into it, but the conservative commentators wanted Carey to remember that prices had also gone down as a consequence. So why not look at it as sort of a raise?

Carey's Timex watch was made in the Philippines. His shirt: Vietnam. His shoes: Indonesia. Those underpants: Indonesia, bro.

Indonesia, Carey said. Seems to be the place.

An old union hand, Carey didn't like Trump much as a person. The Donald had a big mouth, which gave him plenty of room to put his foot in it. But Trump was hitting the high note of the song everyone around here was singing. *Work. We Don't Got None.*

Bernie Sanders was talking a good game too. But Bernie didn't have a shot. The Democratic board was rigged. Hillary controlled the levers of the machine. She had the party on her side. She was in Wall Street's pocket and gave speeches to them, and refused to tell us what she said.

So Carey wasn't about to vote for the establishment, again.

I'm probably gonna end up voting Trump, know what I mean? he said as we took the ten-minute drive around Garbutt. We need jobs. Can you bring jobs? But I don't see how Trump's gonna change Congress or the law. I don't care how good of a negotiator you are. It's too bad, really, you can't put a middle-class person in office.

There were millions of people like Carey in the Rust Belt, people in my family included. We have pride, and we get ornery when someone tells us to fuck off and die. This wasn't about a slobbering white menace or a frothing racist horde. It wasn't a pill-popping population of white self-entitlement. Economic insecurity was the biggest issue in America. It was boring everyday whiskers-in-the-sink white guys like Carey, trying to get by, trying to raise a respectable kid, trying to put something away for retirement. People like Carey felt that the three parties—the Bushes, the Clintons, and the Media—had sold them out. So why not give the bombastic billionaire who railed against Goldman Sachs a shot even if he was friends with Goldman Sachs? What was left to lose?

But the lives of struggling white people don't make good TV, they don't make good copy. They didn't even rate a visit by the media. Trump, to his benefit, figured that much out. He came to Rochester just a few days after I had, the beginning of what would become an eerie pattern. We had been instructed to stop following Trump, but I was getting the freaky feeling Trump was following us.

*Through it all, the public's trust in everything fell to all-time lows.*

*Donald Trump and Hillary Clinton became the least popular characters to seek the presidency in modern history.*

*As for Congress, one imaginative polling firm found that brussels sprouts, head lice, cockroaches, colonoscopies, and gonorrhea were more popular than our elected representatives. Apparently, the American people realized that when you take it up the ass from a proctologist, at least it's for your own well-being. From Congress, not so much.*

*As for the mainstream media, the public's trust in them fell to its lowest level in recorded history. Maybe it was Trump repeatedly calling them out as dishonest. Maybe it was the hyperpartisan posture they'd adopted in the face of an ever-fading audience.*

*Whatever the reason, we had no one to blame but ourselves.*

*The Hillary email leaks during the general election runup confirmed for people what they had long suspected: When it comes to politicians and the press, it's a chummy little dinner party in Washington, D.C.*

*The public got wind of the gaggle of reporters invited to drink, dine, and have an off-the-record conversation at the residence of one of Clinton's campaign representatives; not one of them ever bothered to inform the public of what they heard. Journalists sent unsolicited talking points to her people. They offered obsequious encouragement and slyly provided her questions in advance of a debate. They traded the appearance of independence for access and the occasional but inconsequential scooplet.*

*On the other side, conservative TV pundits were advising Trump on his run, one going so far as to say that he wasn't a journalist at all but a talk show host. What was that supposed to mean? He did no fact checking and tossed questions as soft as overripe cantaloupes? Was Larry King now the gold standard?*

*This went on at the local level as well. At a private birthday party for a government official from which cameras were barred, media personalities nonetheless shamefully posted online pictures of themselves hoisting glasses of booze to the official, all of it paid for by the official's subordinates. These personalities attended conventions and swilled bourbon at kiosks with the contractors, lobbyists, and politicians they were supposed to cover impartially. The contractors, lobbyists, and politicians knew this was good for them. Why else would anyone drink with a reporter?*

*The mass media had become gluttonous for fame. The press awarded themselves prizes and statuettes and reported these as important events to the ordinary citizen. Every year, they threw a big Washington party for themselves where they donned tuxedos and gowns, walked a red carpet, and introduced their sources to movie stars and comedians who played fake reporters better than real reporters played real reporters.*

*And then, as if to repay the favor, real reporters showed up in fictitious movies and TV shows playing their real-life selves reporting fake stories.*

*And former politicos showed up on TV news programs, passing themselves off as independent analysts.*

*You'll forgive the ordinary citizen his confusion.*

*At least a cockroach knows it's always a cockroach.*

# Trail Mix: The Mad Dash to Oblivion in New Brown Shoes

**DETROIT (MARCH)—**

The umpteenth Republican debate was being held in my hometown, so naturally, I was going to be there even if my Trump ban was still in full effect. The networks couldn't get enough of these dung tosses. The ratings were yuuuuge! The final four contestants in the reality show of all reality shows were: Big Don, Little Marco Rubio, Lyin' Ted Cruz, and Doddering John Kasich.

The attendees were party insiders, corpulent white men whose bottom shirt buttons wouldn't keep buttoned, along with their skeleton spouses decorated in pearls and hairspray, and an outlaw biker gang. There went Bill O'Reilly. *Papa Bear!* Christ, he looked like hell without makeup—pallid, the color of a fish's underbelly.

Outside in the blistering cold were a thousand protesters, the New Black Panther Party, New Era Detroit, Black Lives Matter, white hipsters, anarchists. Cops stood with their arms folded, creating a human barricade for the well-dressed white people to scamper inside.

The protesters were loud. Really loud. You could hear their chants and the beating of buckets echoing through the baroque foyer of the Fox Theatre.

*Racist clown get out of town!*

*Dump Trump!*

Black people seemed to universally despise him. Trump had not offended them, not directly anyhow, not as I remembered, but he had offended everybody else from Mexicans to Muslims to those with handicaps, so as far as black people were concerned, he hadn't left much to the imagination.

Still, he was going to need *some* black people to vote for him if he was going to win the White House. Otherwise the numbers didn't add up.

Trump boldly predicted that he would win the black vote. I'm not sure what he meant. Win 51 percent of all blacks who were going to vote? Or win the vote of one single, lonesome, solitary black person? After all, Trump was polling at 0 percent among blacks in some Rust Belt states. To put that in some perspective . . . you can't get lower than 0 percent.

I shouted the question to the Orange Whip after the debate in the ornate hall where the media goat fuck had commenced.

Hey, what are you going to do to get working-class black people into your tent?

He looked at me askance, frowned, and then held his hand up for the entertainment correspondent from *Extra* to inspect. Little

Marco had been suggesting that Trump had smaller-than-average fingers, which meant he probably had smaller-than-average genitalia.

See? Look! Ha! My hands are fine, Big Don crowed. And another thing, I can tell you, *it's* fine. No problems down there.

So I put the race question to his advance guy, George Gigicos, a balding, dumpling-shaped man who served simultaneously as Trump's microphone adjuster, pillow fluffer, and bullet catcher.

You know, Gigicos said, I was thinking the same thing about black people, and I have an idea. I want to pitch him a town hall–style meeting at the Apollo Theater in Harlem.

Really?

Yes, think about it. It's New York, his hometown. And black people there understand him.

Man oh man, I said, handing him my card for the third time that campaign season. That's really gonna work or that's really *not* going to work. Either way, give me a call. I gotta be there.

He promised he would. And then broke his promise.

The Apollo mission never got off the ground. Maybe Chicago had something to do with it. A week after the Detroit debate, Trump's rally at the campus of the University of Illinois at Chicago was called off after a near riot erupted between Trump supporters and protesters. Among the fists and slurs and spitting, a black man bum-rushed the stage, ducking and dodging two beefy white men attempting to detain him. The black man was my old pal Jedidiah Brown, the South Side antiviolence activist now in the middle of the violence, flailing around like Muhammad Ali. I don't blame Brown. Trump was siphoning off all the media attention, and an activist had to do what an activist had to do to get some face time. In any event, Brown had more energy and was more nimble than the Clinton campaign.

FLINT, MICHIGAN (MARCH)—

Bernie and Hillary debated in Flint three days before the Michigan Democratic primary. She had a commanding lead, some pollsters giving her a 99 percent chance of victory. Bernie was an old dishrag as far as the media was concerned: sturdy, useful, but hardly a cocktail conversation piece. Hillary was their woman.

From the outset of the debate, it was obvious that Clinton was taking her talking points from Michael Moore, the left-wing filmmaker and long-gone Flint native son who rediscovered his hometown two long years after it had been poisoned. Flint was a race crime, Clinton insisted, and the ringleader was the Republican governor who had poisoned the black children. And that white governor needed to resign.

I sat watching the debate pregame show in the White Horse Tavern, a local Flint watering hole near the courthouse. I drank beer from the bottle, not wanting to risk dishwater or ice cubes.

Why don't we blame the governor for the horse too, I shouted. I was referring to the giant plastic steed that used to stand on a thirty-foot stanchion out front of the establishment and had blown over the month before.

No doubt, sneered a white woman tending bar.

Politicians of any stripe had few fans among the beleaguered citizens of Flint. Clinton, among the most privileged of white people in America, was making Flint a case of race. Days before the debate had commenced, she had commercials running with her in the pulpit of a local black church.

It's a civil rights issue, she lectured from the blue debate stage. We would be outraged if this happened to white kids, and we should be outraged that it's happening right now to black kids.

Never mind that more than one-third of Flint was white. The bartender's children were white. Clinton was peddling identity politics, stitching together a quilt of minority interests, forgetting that everybody has an identity and grievances. White people had babies too. And they noticed they'd been left out of her talking points.

Bernie the dishrag, who was down 25 percent in some polls, won the Great Lakes State three days later. He even took a third of the Flint vote. It was an upset of stunning and historic proportions. Clearly, there was something wrong with the pollsters, their methodologies, the people they were talking to.

Michigan, a state heavily populated by working people of all colors, was clearly in play. Class was an all-encompassing cloak. Hillary had gotten blown up, but nobody was asking what was up with the polls that had her winning.

### FLORIDA (FEBRUARY/MARCH)—

We were on the I-4 corridor in central Florida, heading toward Daytona. Trump would arrive a week later with the media right behind him. He was getting all the press. Five billion dollars' worth of free airtime. The media was loving him. Before him, nobody was reading or watching a thing. Besides, their gal Hillary had it in the bag. All the polls said so.

*Say something stupid, Don!*

Back in the real world, Danny and Becky were cleaning the infield outhouses the morning after the Daytona 500. Garbage was strewn everywhere. The stench was godawful and turkey buzzards had arrived in the wake.

Becky and Danny, a white couple, did this job every year. They did it without rubber gloves or smocks, earning minimum wage, except Becky didn't know what minimum wage was exactly.

I think it's nine dollars. Innit nine?

No, Danny corrected. It's seven-sixty-seven.

Seven-sixty-seven? Wow, I didn't know that.

Right there, Becky realized she'd taken a 30 percent pay cut.

They were economic refugees, white, undereducated, and there were millions of people like them all over the country feeling like their lives were circling the drain. Danny said he hated both candidates, figuring that nobody was really for people like him anyway. Screw it, he was going for Trump because Hillary wanted to take his health care away, his Obamacare. In short, his pills.

No, you got that wrong, I said. It's Trump who wants to do away with Obamacare.

Oh yeah? Well . . . I still don't like her.

Standing at the threshold of a reeking racetrack shithouse in the mother of all swing states, I wondered. With enough confusion mixed in with the disgust, maybe Trump had a shot in Florida.

Down the highway, in Sanford, nobody was commemorating the fourth anniversary of the death of Trayvon Martin, the unarmed black teenager killed by George Zimmerman, a neighborhood patrol wannabe cop. The boy's death would expose to the world the quiet work done by the NRA. Stand-your-ground laws were now the rule in half the United States, expanding the traditional notion that you could use lethal force to defend yourself inside your house. With the advent of the new laws, you could now kill someone in public in the name of self-defense. The person who usually won these arguments was the one with the gun. It's doubtful that Trayvon knew this. As a consequence of Zimmerman's acquittal, the country was now in the throes of cop versus black.

The entryway to the Retreat at Twin Lakes, the gated community where Martin was slain, was broken, and we drove in without harassment. At the spot where he died, there was no commemorative marker, no flowers, no teddy bear, no news crews. It was quiet and eerie.

The Retreat was an integrated development: whites, blacks, Asians, Hispanics pulling into their garages, the automatic doors closing behind them, the neighbors perfect strangers to one another.

My wife says I can't talk to you, an older black man whom I had shouted out to whispered from an upstairs window, his figure made murky by the screen, his town house the same design as every other town house, the garage door the most prominent feature.

We really don't talk about it around here, he said. It's taboo. Everybody's just trying to get along. We just trying to let it go. Best thing to do, really. For the sake of everybody.

I told him out there in the real world, the silence wasn't working.

## TEXAS (APRIL)—

We headed back to Texas, to the border towns of Brownsville, McAllen, and Laredo. Trump would follow us a few weeks later, pimping his Great Wall. In the meantime, the Central American women and children were back, but in greater numbers now than two years ago, when they were an international spectacle. Now Trump was the international spectacle and the scene on the border was getting little press.

In Laredo, a half dozen Border Patrol agents, all Latinos, were inspecting a narrow drain that led to the banks of the Rio Grande. The sewer was filled with shoes and shirts and other detritus of human movement, and the agents radioed in to HQ to suggest that somebody come out and weld the sewer cap shut. They suspected smugglers may have been ferrying people through the narrow pipe that leads to the riverbank.

The shit's out of control, bro, one of the agents told me. If people out there really knew what was going on. But a wall's not gonna work. You can't build a wall on the river.

In Lynden, Washington, the border with Canada is little more than a ditch. In fact, it is less than a ditch. It is a three-foot culvert bisecting four lanes of country highway. Easy enough to traverse for all Americans threatening to move to Canada should Trump be elected.

But nobody was moving to Canada. It's cold there. Its biggest cities are full of junkies. The health-care system is teetering and the money is made out of plastic; you can actually see right through it. Maybe that's why it lost a quarter of its value.

And what about the eighty thousand Canadians working in the United States illegally? Obviously, the northern border was out of control. Justin Bieber and Ted Cruz—how'd they get in here? Maybe we needed a wall with Canada too.

Inexplicably, a week after we filed this story from the Great White North, Trump showed up to the one-horse town on the western edge of the 49th parallel for a rally, touting his Great Mexican Wall.

Weird. We were starting to think his campaign had a mole in our office.

**DETROIT (MAY)—**

Detroit mayor Mike Duggan was at it again. I tweeted the following 108 characters on my personal account.

*One thing I learned today. The FBI has an open and ongoing investigation into the Detroit demolition program.*

The following day, it was the above-the-fold headline of both of the city's daily newspapers. The poor newspapers. Nobody even bought them for birdcage lining anymore. As for TV, it never ran the story.


CLEVELAND (JULY)—


The morning news on July 18 was awful: cops ambushed in Baton Rouge, three dead and three wounded. Add to that the five officers killed by an Army veteran in Dallas earlier in the month. The headlines came instantaneously: *Baton Rouge Shootings Could Cast a Pall over the Republican National Convention.*

Hardly.

The Big Bubble machine was in town, fifteen thousand media types nearly doubling the police and military personnel brought to Cleveland, Ohio, to protect them in their made-for-TV cocoon. The parabolic dishes, high-definition cameras, shotgun mics, and the oppressive heat gave the feeling of hot gas being cranked through a giant calliope.

The gentry media seemed blissfully unaware of the depths of the discord in American life bubbling outside the protective envelope. Inside the perimeter, they wandered aimlessly in their expensive suits. Brown shoes seem to be the style of the moment for the male political media.

A couple of agents from the Secret Service and I stood at the bottom of the escalator of the media center, admiring the footwear. The colors ranged from saddle tan to walnut, khaki, camel, cappuccino, cognac, caramel, burnished brown, dark burgundy brown, tobacco, tan, café, and beach sand.

The leather styles included high sheen, flat, gloss, grainy, antique, vintage, and the prefab distressed look. There was a little something for every man: the lace-up loafer, the cap toe oxford, the bike toe oxford, and, not to be outdone, the snub toe oxford. There went the classic wingtip (both dimpled and smooth), the extra-long wingtip, the monk strap buckle, the Piccadilly loafer and its lower-class cousin, the penny loafer. Hey look, buddy, there's the perforated cap toe lace-up! Imported from Italy. Made in India.

I guess they must get paid pretty well in TV, one agent surmised.

They're not getting paid for originality, said the other.

T he discussions in the media hall were not intellectual ones about the base of malcontent in America or the reasons for the rise of Trump, but rather over who got the last bagel at the breakfast buffet or who was up next at the makeup mirror. Women waddled around in curlers and bathrobes, readying themselves for their segments on the gigantic blue homecoming float that served as the network set. The lesser lights of local TV news were assigned table space off to the side and on the floor.

In the hallway, members of the neocon cabal that brought you the Iraq War were whispering and laughing among themselves. *How bad is this thing with Roger Ailes?* They were older, redder, chubbier, and brown-shoed now, but they were still hanging around, posing on TV as men who had answers. How the fuck were they still hanging around? I wondered. Who let them in?

There was the black sheriff of Milwaukee who was fond of denying the existence of police brutality in America, walking around in beads and jeans and a straw cowboy hat curled at the brim. Jesus, at least he wasn't wearing the brown shoes.

This was nowhere, man. Looking to get outside the bubble, Matt and I drove to the west side of town, where Tamir Rice, a twelve-year-old black boy who had been brandishing a pellet gun, was shot dead by police two days before Ferguson would burn for the second time.

It wasn't a particularly deep idea, and I'd expected dozens of news crews to be out there, the makeshift picnic-table memorial under a gazebo in the park where he died, with its votive candles and helium balloons providing a somber and natural backdrop to the riot barricades and klieg lights at the convention's perimeter. Thankfully there was not one other reporter there. Not one camera. Just a solitary, slightly built black man sitting on a bench, smoking a menthol.

He was wearing his uniform from the morning shift at the fast-food joint where he worked the griddle for $8.15 an hour. After the government extracted its taxes from his biweekly check, it took him an hour to earn breakfast where he worked. So he stole his breakfast. His ball cap was creased and frayed at the brim, his black battered tennis shoes stained with sugar and syrup drippings from doughnuts and flavored coffees.

You can't say them cops in Louisiana deserved it, he said. That was a straight-up ambush. But what about the boy here? Tamir? A toy gun? Cop didn't say nothing to him. Just jumps outta the car and starts blasting. What side, whose side, you supposed to be on with shit like that happening every day?

What side are you on? I asked.

He pointed toward the road. Two hundred feet away stood an obelisk to fallen Cleveland police officer Jonathan Schroeder, a white man shot and killed ten years earlier attempting to arrest the rapist of a black woman he had never met.

What side you want me to be on? he asked.

I didn't know there had to be a side, I said.

Oh, you always got to pick a side. Sometimes, you just change the side you pick.

DETROIT (JULY)—

I picked the side of never again attending a political convention. I canceled my trip to the Democratic Party's coronation of Hillary Clinton in Philadelphia and returned to Detroit to catch final arguments and jury deliberation for Barry Ellentuck, the demolition whistleblower.

What was to be gained in Philly? Leaked emails from top Democratic National Committee officials revealed what we already knew: The game was fixed and played in a tub of filth. The party belonged to the Clintons. One top official had gone so far as to suggest that the party ought to weaponize Sanders's Jewish heritage against him.

Bernie had no one to blame for his close loss but himself, really. His campaign lacked specificity and detail. He refused to pound Clinton as a conniving, dishonest establishment power grubber, a side switcher who would cynically alter her worldview to fit the latest polling data on things like globalism, Wall Street, world trade, and law and order in the urban cores. In the end, Bernie chose courtesy and capitulation while thousands of his supporters were outside the convention center as President Obama spoke. They were shouting: *Fuck Hillary Clinton!*

Back in Detroit, Ellentuck was another man being ground to pulp in the gearbox of the Clinton machine. The man had been virtually destroyed by the charges of attempting to defraud the city a few thousand dollars of federal demolition funds. No one in the construction industry would touch a man at war with the sitting

Democratic mayor of Detroit who had close ties to Hillary Clinton. If convicted of anything, Ellentuck was done forever.

The jury came back in three hours, which included lunch. Ellentuck was found not guilty of attempting to defraud the government of $6,000. Despite the verdict, his wife stewed in the gallery. The whole ordeal could have been avoided had the prosecutor bothered to interview Ellentuck, who, suspecting a setup, secretly recorded the government's key witnesses contradicting their sworn testimony. It was an embarrassment for the young prosecutor, who left the courtroom without comment. But not for long. He was appointed by the governor three months later to the bench of the Third Judicial Circuit Court of Michigan, his courtroom directly above the judge who served strawberry danish.

Two days after Ellentuck's acquittal, Mayor Duggan was onstage at the Philadelphia convention extolling the virtues of Crooked Hillary. He was said to be in line for a position in her cabinet, perhaps as secretary of Housing and Urban Development or Veterans Affairs. No media, local or national, asked why Clinton had invited a figure of a federal corruption probe to speak on her behalf. To me, it went to the root of everything wrong.

All I could do was tweet it.

MILWAUKEE, WISCONSIN (AUGUST)—

Just a few days after the convention, a corner of black Milwaukee went up in flames. This time it was a black cop killing a black suspect carrying a stolen handgun and five hundred rounds of ammunition in his rental car. The suspect, Sylville Smith, ran with the weapon and the official story at the time was that the cop feared for his life.

The dead man's father apologized to TV for not being a better role model. At the scene of Smith's death, his adopted mother told me Smith and the cop knew each other, that the killing was the result, perhaps, of a beef over a baby mama.

Probably not a baby mama. On the second night of disorder, the officer, Dominique Heaggan-Brown, allegedly sat in a bar with a man he met on Facebook watching live TV footage of the burning corner, bragging that he could do whatever he wanted without repercussion. Heaggan-Brown was later charged with taking the man home and raping him.

And he was also charged with homicide in Smith's shooting death after body-cam footage showed that Heaggan-Brown shot Smith as he pursued him between two houses. Heaggan-Brown put a second bullet in Smith's chest a second and a half later, after Smith had thrown his gun over a fence and had his hands over his head on the ground. Prosecutors called the first bullet justified; the second, murder. The jury disagreed. Haeggan-Brown was acquitted.

It took flames to get the public's attention, said James Flippin, a barber at the Sho'Nuff shop just down the way from the gas station rubble on Burleigh Street. But the flames didn't come until TV came, he said.

It's a script in America now, he went on. Now it's like okay, come on, dog, come up here. Lights, camera, action. We on the news. Wanna be seen. Wanna be heard.

But nobody was really listening. Not a single elected official showed up to the corner. Not the white Democratic mayor, not the tough-talking suburban cowboy sheriff, not the white Republican governor. Not Hillary Clinton. It was obvious they were afraid of their own people.

As for Donald Trump, the Republican nominee came into town while the embers on the north side were still warm. Well, he didn't actually come into town. Not even into Milwaukee County. He showed up twenty-five miles away in suburban West Bend, finally making his pitch to black America in front of a nearly unanimously white, if confused, audience.

His pitch was simple, one I tried to tell him months ago: Why not vote for me? What have you got to lose?

FLINT, MICHIGAN (SEPTEMBER)—

Trump tried this for a month or so, addressing black America in front of white America, TV's airwaves serving as a stand-in for his lack of courage.

Then he arrived in Flint for a tour of the water treatment plant and what I believe was his first address to an actual real-life group of black people at a local church.

Coincidentally, I too was in Flint. It was like we were running mates or something. New York, Florida, Washington, Wisconsin, and now Michigan. Just weird. I had come to town with a stall of showers and a chromium gasoline tanker full of fresh water from Ann Arbor, filming a bit with a filmmaker friend about the lack of progress on the water-poisoning situation. The mayor's office had granted me a permit to set up the showers in front of city hall, but realizing the optics of that, they rescinded their permission. Angry, I barged into city hall demanding a refund of my $25 permit fee.

I was informed by a telephone call from the mayor's staff that the police had been notified about my refusal to leave city hall and that my water tanker was occupying parking spaces illegally. I was also informed in a second telephone call that Trump had landed at the airport and was on his way to the water plant. Imagine the scene: the cops chasing me in a chromium water tanker while I chased Trump in my chromium water tanker around the city.

We dodged the police, missed Trump's motorcade, but got to the church in time to see Trump drive away. His talk had been cut short by the pastor because Big Don was talking smack about Crooked Hillary.

In the parking lot, I ran into Sam Riddle, my favorite ex-con political operator, who had gone to prison for his role in the Detroit corruption scandal a few years earlier.

Why not? Riddle said of Trump. Why not? Hillary came and pimped us and all we got was some bottled water. So why not let Trump come pimp us too? Why not?

## DETROIT (SEPTEMBER)—

While I was in Flint, Detroit police sergeant Ken Steil was shot and wounded attempting to arrest a madman who had carjacked multiple people, shot his own father, and threatened to kill his own mother.

Five days later Sergeant Steil was dead from a blood clot, making him the fortieth police officer in America in 2016 to die in the line of duty. I knew Steil, first introduced to him when we tailed his special operations unit on the streets of Detroit for a bankruptcy story about the city and its effect on police.

Let me say that if bad cops were truly the problem in urban America, then men like Ken Steil were certainly the solution. He was the squad leader of an elite unit that hunted the worst of humanity: rapists, murderers of children, the criminally insane. His crew often found themselves in dark alleyways and abandoned houses, the only light yielded by shards of moonlight through shattered rooftops.

In his twenty years on the job, Steil had never discharged his firearm and had no discipline or misconduct complaints of any kind in his file. He died trying to catch a man who had tried to murder his own father and was rampaging across the city with a shotgun. Someone called the police and Sergeant Steil answered. No questions asked. And now he was dead.

I called his men to offer my condolences, but decided to stay away from his widow, JoAnn. That is the proper thing for a newsperson to do. I had learned a long time ago, in the aftermath of 9/11, that a reporter knocking on the door of a grieving family was nothing more than emotional acetone, which will erode what little glue is left holding it together.

But I got a call from JoAnn, through one of her husband's colleagues. She wished to see me. There was something she wanted to tell the world, I was told. So Matt and I pulled up and parked a few houses down from hers, a respectable distance so the family and friends might have a few moments to see us and adjust to our presence. The police department had a ceremonial car parked out front of her home, the hood peeling, an oversized dartboard of rust located where the decal used to be. A fucking joke.

The mood in the house was somber, the two little boys taken to school by Steil's brothers in blue. Against the far wall was a saltwater fish tank he had built. JoAnn laughed softly, saying she had no idea how to care for it, but she'd try.

Matt readied the camera and she took a deep, quaking breath:

I forgive the person who did this to him, she said, because I know in my heart, if he knew what he took from us, he wouldn't have done this. We need more love in this country right now.

My heart ached as it had not in many years. A widow forgives her husband's murderer. She then asks us all to love one another. And yet who showed her and her children love? At the funeral, Steil was given a posthumous promotion to captain. It was good for the cameras, but it came with no increase in pension benefits for his wife and children. Financially, he would still be a sergeant. And because of the city's bankruptcy, his family would no longer receive health coverage. Through the power of the woman's grace projected into the living rooms of lawmakers, however, the state of Michigan granted Joann and her children health-care benefits . . . for five years. When the oldest boy turned ten, he'd have to fend for himself.

Most insulting was the matter of the funeral bill. Despite its pomp and circumstance, and the mayor in attendance spouting crime statistics over his casket, the funeral of Steil would not be paid for by the city he died serving, but rather by the family he left behind.

If there was a war on police in America, it felt like the snipers were on every side: criminals, activists, double-talking politicians, commentators. But instead of war, a widow called for love. And all I could do for her with the power of TV was scrounge together five measly years of pediatrician visits.

Her words—her situation, the faces of her small boys—emotionally cracked me. Her husband kept his end of the bargain, to serve. The politicians, the lawyers and the bankers did not, they took. And it was too late for Steil to break the contract. Another crushing example of the giant gulf between a government and its people, between races, between classes. It was all so tantalizingly clear: the white man in Garbutt and a cop's widow in Detroit, the black man in the streets of Ferguson and the Latina woman polishing the Gipper's marble in Simi Valley had so much in common but could not find a common ground. And this thing called TV only served to spin confusion. I'd absorbed the disorder as if it were gasoline vapors. It was corrosive. I needed air. I needed to get out.

SOUTHFIELD, MICHIGAN (NOVEMBER)—

I may have been the national correspondent, the man on the American street for the giant media company, but election night was for men in brown shoes on a blue set. Housecats, we called them. There was nothing for me to do, really, but I came to the Detroit station anyway, should someone want my perspective.

Not that they would need any. Hillary Clinton had this in the bag. All the polls and media outlets had been saying it for months. I wasn't so sure.

A colleague of mine was doing a Facebook live bit from the newsroom, ostensibly to show the station's followers the goings-on of a harried journalistic barnyard on election night. He wandered over and asked me how I thought the evening would shake out, what with me having been out *there.*

From my perspective, having crisscrossed this great land, black people had their man in Obama. He was something aspirational, uplifting, hopeful, but in that eight years, their lives had not improved appreciably. And now that he was gone, there was little incentive for them to show up in the same numbers for Clinton. As for Latinos, I remembered my time in California. Even if an illegal immigrant looks like you, has a similar-sounding name, he's still going to look different if you have to compete with him for a livelihood. Working-class white people? Some thought they finally had a guy in Trump. He was not the reflection of hate in white people, he was a reaction to the state of distress inflicted upon them by an establishment that either manipulated them, took them for granted, or ignored them altogether.

There was too much *They* and not enough *Us*. We were all saying the same thing—we were all worried for our children, and yet we couldn't hear each other above the shouting and the shattering glass and the ambulance horns. Nobody expected anything to change regardless of the evening's outcome. But yes, I told my colleague. You're going to be surprised at the vote. Michigan and the Rust Belt were in play. Self-interest never seems to be quite what the media thinks it is.

I didn't predict Trump would win—only a backstretch rummy trying to win it all back on the long shot would consider putting his money down on the star of a "pussy grabber" video. It's worth remembering, women are not a minority.

But I did think the vote would be razor close. The polls, I believed, had it wrong. It wasn't that people were afraid to say they were voting for Trump. I just think they hated pollsters and reporters. And pollsters, like too many reporters, work the phones instead of the streets.

I went back to my office in the back of the building, separated from the blue news set by a cinder-block wall. I turned on the TV. Then I took out the bottle of vodka from my desk drawer that had been given to me by a guest from one of the many cooking segments the station produces, got some stale ice from the staff refrigerator, and put my feet up.

The anchors' and pundits' faces grew longer with horror as each hour of the evening unfolded. It was obvious to everyone that they had been reporting on the country not as it was, but as they imagined it to be.

Around two in the morning, it was done. I rinsed my glass, swept the photographs from my desk into my satchel, and went home. I had a daughter to get off to school in the morning.

**2017**

# Tighty Whities

I spent Year One of Our Trump in my underpants, at my writing desk, in an office overlooking the expressway.

Tired and dispirited, I tried to avoid the shitshow altogether: I left the TV job. I followed no one on Twitter. I tuned out cable news. I poured my energy into these pages. Even so, the media delirium seeped in through the floorboards like pus from a boil.

I admit it, I was a fish to the clickbait. The clichéd and melodramatic outrage depressed me, but still I couldn't help but watch. Each morning, I'd lock myself away, wearing nothing but yesterday's underpants, unshaven and unbrushed, procrastinating on my laptop. Like most everyone else in America, I was now only a virtual participant in the national debate, a househusband with his soap opera, a caged commodity held captive by the social media platforms.

I watched live-stream press conferences with amusement and a nagging melancholy brought on by unemployment and a lack of action. Trump and the media. What was it today? One of his Or-angeness's whoppers? Biggest inauguration crowd ever? Obama had him wiretapped? Or the inane: Big Don is afraid of houseflies? Two-dollar Donny thinks the White House is a dump? (He ought to be thankful he's not staying at the Trump International in Las Ve-gas. #Shithole!) Why was Melania wearing stilettos to a hurricane? Or the deadly serious: Did Trump obstruct justice when he fired FBI director James Comey? Did his campaign collude with Russian intelligence agents? Did he bumble his way into an obstruction charge? Will he be impeached? Will he bomb North Korea's Little Rocket Man?

Some of these things were important. But it was hard to gauge their order since they were all given loud volume and wide play. It was good for ratings and clicks, but too much of it had little to do with the daily struggles of the American people.

Trump and his petty lies and his petty handlers calling his petty lies "facts" caused Orwell's opus *1984* to resurface onto the best-seller list. In this futurist parable about a dystopian totalitarian society, hate ruled and whatever the leader said was true—was true.

But I sat in my office, instead reading Huxley's *Brave New World*. It seemed more fitting to me. In this future world, the party bosses, their bureaucrats, and newspaper editors and the pharma-ceutical manufacturers conspired to teach the masses to love their enslavement by giving the people exactly what they think they wanted: limitless and empty entertainment, free sex, and plentiful narcotics. It was a kinder, more sinister oppression. A place where freedom is lost without the citizen ever realizing it. A shitshow, in short.

No doubt, the tenor of political conversation had become harder and more shrill since Trump hit the political scene, but I thought I could hear a familiar echo through my headphones. Many of the

white supremacists who marched with tiki torches in Charlottesville, Virginia, protesting the removal of the statue of Confederate
general Robert E. Lee, for instance, were the same people I'd en-
countered two years earlier when I took that moonlight drive with
the Grand Dragon of the KKK to Columbia, South Carolina. As sad
and despicable as Charlottesville was, there were a few hundred of
these white supremacists. Not thousands, or tens of thousands, or
hundreds of thousands. Not an army. The media could estimate the
millions who attended presidential inaugurations from aerial photographs, it seemed, but could not do a simple head count of a troop
of racist orangutans. Shitshow.

In the things that matter in everyday lives, very little changed
in a practical way: There was still a lack of good jobs, wages were
still too low, the cost of health care was growing higher, the
treatment of veterans was abysmal. There were the unaddressed
matters of the budget deficit, the national debt, corporate welfare,
failing pension systems, unaffordable tuition, and a broken immigration system.

Trump's breakfast-time tweets and revolving cast of insiders
whose names are certain to be lost to history aside, Goldman Sachs
and the Joint Chiefs of Staff still ran the White House. Special interests still ruled Congress. And the taxpayers still subsidized the
Senate gymnasium and sauna. (Ironically, it is a members-only
gymnasium, thus making it the only certain place in Washington,
D.C., where you will not see a lobbyist performing a rubdown on a
member of Congress.)

Here in Detroit, the administration of Democratic mayor Mike
Duggan received rave reviews from the national press corps, despite the fact that the neighborhoods were still crime-ravaged
shooting galleries. Reporters would parachute into town for a mo-
jito at the newest downtown bistro, take a quick ride on the new

light rail, conduct a deskside interview with Hizzoner, and pronounce the place "Comeback City." Much of the local print media, hollowed out by staffing cuts and a diminishing readership, were happy to promote the simple Huxleyesque narrative, and TV news simply copied their headlines. There were no stories about a federal grand jury corruption probe into the city's demolition program. I had to tweet it in my underpants. At this writing, its investigation was still ongoing.

As for Flint, the governor's people pronounced the water officially safe to drink, but few people believed it. The governor himself never showed his face in Vehicle City again to drink from the taps, while residents were now required to pay full cost for the water.

In the cities of Chicago, Baltimore, and St. Louis, murder spiked as police officers slowed their work. It is worth noting that no police officer has been convicted for the illegal use of deadly force in any incident in this book, and nationally, two have been convicted since 2013. It's also worth noting that since the events of Ferguson, about fifty law-enforcement officers across the United States have been ambushed and killed.

In the South, industrial workers continued to reject union representation, overwhelmingly voting it down at a Nissan plant in Mississippi and a Boeing factory in South Carolina. In the meantime, labor officials plead guilty to accepting bribes form Fiat-Chrysler executives in exchange for company-friendly positions at the bargaining table.

In the West, Jon Ritzheimer, the half-cocked, pistol-packing "patriot," pleaded guilty to conspiracy for his role in Oregon and was sentenced to one year and one day in federal prison. He remains recalcitrant, however, calling the government illegitimate and himself the Rosa Parks of the West. Booda, the fake sniper, also pleaded guilty, serving nine months in jail. The conspiracy trial of Cliven Bundy and his sons for their role in the Bunkerville takeover was declared a mistrial, after a judge ruled that government lawyers had intentionally withheld evidence that could have helped in their defense. The men cannot be retried, and the government is now investigating its lawyers.

Shitshow.

In the North, Junior the white kid from Garbutt did not pick up the heroin needle as predicted. Instead, he followed his father's advice, finished high school, and enrolled in community college, where he studies to be a paramedic. The military recruiters still stop by.

In the Midwest, I tried to find DJ, the brave young black man from Ferguson, Missouri, who tried unsuccessfully to save the Arab's liquor store. He vanished as far as anybody in Ferguson knew. I suspect he's living a life and raising his son. I think that, because that's what real men do.

In the workplace, a cascade of prominent men were fired for allegations of sexual harassment. Roger Ailes, after being pushed out of Fox with a $40 million severance, slipped and fell in his private residential bathroom, struck his head, and died. May God rest him.

Bill O'Reilly was the next to go, followed by movie mogul Harvey Weinstein, followed by a host of male power brokers in media, entertainment, and politics. Through it all, Trump, the man accused of snatching a score of women and bragging about it on videotape, held tightly to the highest chair in the land.

Reporters were now shouting questions at the president that would have gotten them fired just months ago.

*Sir, are you a racist?*

Spinning-in-the-spinroom was ahead of its time.

. . .

Things were a mess. It felt as if the country had come loose from its moorings, and Washington was consumed by its own navel. But maybe there was a silver lining in it. Whenever Washington does manage to get "big things" done, the American people get whipsawed. The price of homes collapses. Jobs leave for Mexico. Trickle-down never seems to trickle down, while the roads fall apart. Like NAFTA or the war in Iraq, the consequences of the one thing Congress did get done—the mega eleventh-hour tax cuts—will not be known without the long lens of time. So maybe stalemate is the best medicine for what ails us as we try to catch our collective breath, collect the pieces of a broken future, and figure a path for our children.

It is dispiriting, though, to stare into the screen and then get up and go to the bathroom and stare into the toilet bowl and realize everything is headed in the same direction. We're rafting down a sewer where the scenery never changes. The rich get richer. The poor get children. And the anchorman feigns outrage.

*Ladies and gentlemen: we return you to our regular programming.*

# Afterword: Black Tar
# and White Noise

I now work as a handyman at a downtown Detroit diner. I plunge toilets clogged by constipated junkies. I scrape grease from days gone by. I vacuum mummified hot dogs. This morning, I am on my knees repairing and painting the foundation where the walls meet the sidewalk.

Often people recognize me from my time as a TV reporter. The cops, the bus drivers, the construction workers, the priests, the housewives, even the former emergency manager who steered Detroit through its historic bankruptcy. He is a big fan of the hot dogs here.

What the hell you doing down there?

Working, I said. What's it look like?

Didn't know you types had it in you, he said, laughing.

Someone in the media has to get his loafers dirty.

Like the actor bagging groceries at a New Jersey supermarket who got outed on social media—the guy used to appear on *The Cosby Show*—I get job-shamed sometimes. I've been reduced to physical labor. One smart ass from the East Coast wrote "Former Pulitzer Winner Falls on Hard Times."

Even the top manservant for the mayor of Detroit recently wrote that my career was "deteriorating badly."

Maybe. Or maybe I'm still waiting for those criminal indictments to come crashing down on Hizzoner's administration, while I continue to track and report about him and his machine on one of those scrappy local websites that is supposed to fill the void of the disappearing newspapers. They don't like me in City Hall or the White House for that matter. But that doesn't hurt my feelings any. I keep scraping gum from the sidewalk. I'm patient. And so is democracy.

Out here. Down here, valuable things can be learned about real life in an American City.

The dusty work boots tell me there is a real estate bubble. Money is cheap to borrow. Federal short term interest rates are lower than inflation. That means you make money by borrowing money and make more by getting the public bank to kick in on development projects. That's profit without even trying. And now the entire downtown has become an "Opportunity Zone" under the Trump tax law—that means downtown has become a tax haven, a place for the very rich to park their capital gains to avoid paying taxes.

As a consequence, there is a building boom downtown, despite the fact that the city's population continues to drop and wages continue to fall when inflation is taken into account and banking jobs are factored out. Stacking the money, the hard hats in work boots tell me. General Motors is closing its very last factory based in Detroit. Imagine that? The stock market is up and down like a washwoman's ass.

The bottom will drop out, a road worker told me. It always does.

And while the billionaire developers get billions in public subsidies, the lunatics maraud the streets in numbers I've never seen before. I keep my head on a swivel. These wretches have no medication, no place to sleep but the occasional cot in the county jail. One madman recently tried to hang himself by stripping his belt from his trouser loops, wrapping it around his neck, and holding himself up by his arms. This, he eventually realized, defied the law of physics. He was sent on his way with a box of warm food and a tasty slice of pie.

Let him eat cake! Government investment in the care of the deranged is shrinking because we're told there isn't enough money.

It is dirty on the street. There are needles, stale Band-Aids, and the occasional semi-rare penny. But it's the cigarettes that get me. Good economic times would suggest that they occasionally go half-smoked. The more money, the longer the cigarette butt. That's how it is on Wall Street. But people here in Detroit do not feel rich, if their cigarette debris is to be believed. They smoke their Newport 100s and Winston Lights down to the butt. I don't care what the Consumer Confidence Index says. The Cigarette Barometer tells me people are expecting a rough ocean ahead.

Monday is the worst day. That's trash pickup day. The chicken bones and onion boxes litter the streets and bums paw through them. Garbage collection, I've noticed, is increasingly tardy, since one of the main trash haulers in the city was caught up in a cash-for-contract bribery scandal. Some things never change around here.

And then again, some things do change. The first Monday of the month is worse than your average Monday. The government checks come then. People get high, flop out at the bus stop, and mutter to themselves. This fuels the disconnect between the destitute and the new brown shoe crowd and the hipster hurtling around on rental scooters. I ain't gonna hurt you, the poor man complains as the rich man walks widely around him. I'm a human being.

The head of the political beast may be in Washington, D.C. But the heart and stomach of that beast are here in the middle of the country: places like Detroit and Chicago and St. Louis. Capitol Hill is the clubhouse where the spoils are divided and taken home, but here on the street you don't taste it. Consider that Detroit went bankrupt in order to provide better public safety. But the bullets still fly, and the police are taking jobs in suburban jurisdictions where the pay is better. While on my knees the other morning, a cop blared to a motorist over his loudspeaker: You're blocking traffic, move the car. The motorist ignored him. The cop again: Move your car or I'll ticket you for expired plates. It was a barter. The cop was too busy. The motorist was too poor. Where else does that happen? The motorist moved his car.

Still, Detroit is an excellent place. And so is America. Cosmopolitan and diverse. A world destination despite all its troubles, past and present. That's why the lines are long at the Mexican consulate on Fort Street. Here on this corner, automobiles roll by blaring all sorts of music: Arabic, Latin, Bengali, Greek, Hip Hop, and Classic Rock all banging up on each other. Troubles, yes. The end of days?

No matter what the television and Internet are telling you, I don't hear a beef among the people down here at the street level. Only the call for "spare change."

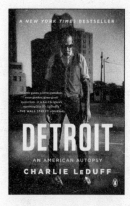

## DETROIT
### An American Autopsy

With the steel-eyed reportage that has become his trademark, and the righteous indignation only a native son possesses, Charlie LeDuff sets out to uncover what precipitated Detroit's slide from one of the richest cities in America to a place devastated by hardship.

## US GUYS
### The True and Twisted Mind of the American Man

US Guys is LeDuff's odyssey in search of the truth behind the American man. With audacity, humor, and no small amount of physical pain, he captures a broad diversity of voices as they wrestle with an America they love but increasingly fail to understand.

"Fearless, clear-eyed." –Entertainment Weekly

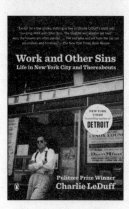

## WORK AND OTHER SINS
### Life in New York City and Thereabouts

In Work and Other Sins, LeDuff gives his incomparable take on New York City and its denizens. The result is at turns a riotous, dirt-under-the-nails vision of life in the Big Apple and beyond.

"Blunt and touching . . . The laughter and wisdom are hard won." –The New York Times Book Review